Published in The United States in 1999 by
Contemporary Books
A division of NTC/Contemporary Publishing
Group, Inc.
4255 West Touhy Avenue
Lincolnwood (Chicago), Illinois 60646-1975 U.S.A.

ISBN 0-8092-2592-1
Text copyright © 1999 by Emi Kazuko
Design and layout copyright © 1999 by
Conran Octopus Ltd
Photography copyright © 1999 by Jeremy Hopley

Managing Editor Kate Bell
Editorial Assistant Tanya Robinson
Copy Editor Norma MacMillan
Editorial Consultant Jenni Muir

Art Editor Alison Fenton
Stylist Wei Tang
Food for Photography Meg Jansz
Typesetting Olivia Norton

Picture Research Liz Boyd
Production Julian Deeming

Cataloging-in-Publication Data is available from the
United States Library of Congress
Printed and bound in Hong Kong

Page 1 *Assorted Tempura (page 47)*
Pages 2–3 *Grilled Skewered Chicken (page 38)*
Pages 4–5 *Fruit Salad with Kanten and Adzuki Paste
(page 124)*

café

japan

Emi Kazuko

Photography by Jeremy Hopley

CONTEMPORARY BOOKS

Contents

Introduction

Japan is a nation of food lovers and restaurant-goers. Whereas in the West, friends or colleagues might say "let's *get together*"—which often means just for a drink—in Japan, the irresistible invitation is "let's go and eat something delicious." And that always means going to a restaurant, possibly followed by a drink or two at a bar. Indeed, the Japanese eat out a lot more frequently than the average Westerner goes to a pub. For the Japanese, the restaurant is an extension of their home dining room, so it's quite natural for people to go out for a meal two or three times a week. This is true for all ages, from 8 to 80.

The range of restaurants is enormous, from *ryotei*, top-quality *kaiseki* (banquet) restaurants, to more modest restaurants offering home cooking, where the menu changes daily. Here they serve down-to-earth food that is nostalgically described as "mother's taste"—such as boiled rice and *miso* soup with grilled fish and pickled vegetables for breakfast, chicken and egg rice bowls for lunch, and again rice and *miso* soup with beef and vegetable casserole for supper. Each restaurant has its own cooking style, and every day fresh ingredients are brought from the markets and cooked on the premises, often by a husband and wife team, with their children helping to serve. They take the utmost pride in what they cook and present.

Small bistros or cafés that specialize in only one dish or ingredient are a unique feature of Japan's food culture. People do not say "let's go to a Japanese restaurant," but instead "let's go and eat *sushi*," and then pick a *sushi* restaurant. The choices are endless—*Tempura*, *Yakitori*, *soba*, *ramen*, *Kabayaki* (grilled eel), *Tonkatsu* (fried pork cutlet), hotpot dishes, *Teppanyaki* (griddles), and *Oden* (hotpot of assorted fish cakes) all have their own individual restaurants. There are not only general fish restaurants, where they serve fish and shellfish of the season, but also restaurants specializing in a particular species of fish. One such is *fugu* (globefish), which is frequently talked about in the West because parts of it are poisonous (chefs require a special license to handle it).

The Japanese always eat while drinking—it's a matter of wonder for them how Westerners can drink alcohol without eating any proper food—and at drinking places, the food accompanying the *sake* or Scotch matters as much as the drink itself. Every bar, whether a Japanese-style *koryoriya* ("small dishes" bar) or a Western-style bar or beer hall, serves its own freshly made food. In such places it's normal for small hors d'oeuvre dishes, such as *nameko* mushrooms with grated *daikon*, cucumber and *wakame* vinaigrette, or bean sprouts and shrimp salad, to be served automatically as you sit down at the counter or table.

Bars display the day's seasonal specialties on the wall, or else the *itamae* (Japanese counter chef) or *mama-san* (bar manageress) will tell you what good fish or vegetables they bought at the market that morning. If you are a regular customer, they may even serve you something very special that is not listed on the board.

The Japanese love of food is evident at home, too. Every night, at least three different dishes will be presented on the dinner table, from which the family members help themselves to eat with their individual bowls of rice and soup. Though more and more Japanese women go out to work, the majority still stay at home to look after the family, and their main concern is food. As they shop for fresh produce every day, local small specialty food shops, rather than distant supermarkets, are vital for them. Markets are found not in the streets, but in the basement floors of department stores. Inside such ultra-modern buildings, old-fashioned market trading takes place every day. It's an amazing sight, with the accompanying smells of fresh produce, fish, and meat, and loud shouts of *"rasshai, rasshai"* to cajole shoppers into sampling products.

Geographically, Japan is a long, narrow country, stretching down 16 latitudes, whose produce from sea and land varies enormously, from salmon and crab from Hokkaido in the north to tuna from Kyushu in the south. In addition, Japan has one of the most balanced climates in the world, with the year equally divided into the four seasons, so it is quite natural that the freshly grown fruits and vegetables of particular climates, or the seasonal catch of a particular fish, often make up a region's specialty dish. Even rice has its regional differences, with every rice-growing region developing its own type, complete with a fancy brand name. Regional variations in ingredients and cooking persist very strongly.

The essence of Japanese cooking lies in its simplicity. The Japanese believe that simplicity is the best, if not the only, way to bring out the natural flavors and textures of fresh ingredients, not to alter or disguise them, and at the same time to retain their natural appearance. As a result, Japanese cooking is very easy, often embarrassingly so. Vegetables are only just cooked, so they keep their crunchiness, or salted to take the "chill" out of them. Fish is often eaten raw, or cured with vinegar, lightly grilled, or quickly fried. Meat is used sparingly, both because of the old Buddhist vegetarian tradition and also because of its extremely high price, and is almost always thinly sliced and cooked with vegetables.

In this book, many of the most popular Japanese daily dishes are presented. You do not need any special skill or knowledge to cook them, and they use ingredients that are readily available at supermarkets and Asian markets in the West. In trying them you will find that they capture the essence of this country's food: just heed what nature is offering, as they say in Japan.

The Japanese pantry

Vegetables and fruits

Adzuki beans (azuki) *Tiny, hard red adzuki beans are used mainly to make sweet bean paste (an) for desserts. Ready-made* an *is obtainable in powdered or paste form.*

Daikon *A large, long, white radish (also called* mooli, rettich, *and Chinese icicle radish), this is probably the most widely used vegetable in Japan. It is often grated and used raw to make sauces, or sliced and cooked as a vegetable. When pickled it is called* takuan.

Hakusai *Although known in English as Napa cabbage, this cabbage is Japanese in origin. Hakusai is often salted to take the "chill," or hard rawness, out of it and bring out the flavor.*

Kabocha squash *This Japanese variety of winter squash is sold in many supermarkets. The flesh is dense and full of flavor, so no seasoning is necessary.*

Konnyaku *A grayish-brown jelly-like cake made from yam flour, this is eaten mainly for its gelatinous texture. It is supposed to cleanse the stomach. Konnyaku is available fresh in packets at Japanese supermarkets.*

Satoimo *Although sometimes called a potato, this dark, hairy-skinned vegetable is, in fact, a type of yam, related to eddoes and taro root. It is the shape and size of a light bulb. The flesh is dense and fine in texture, with a flavor that is slightly different from Western potatoes.*

Shiitake mushrooms *Among the many Japanese varieties of mushroom, shiitake is the best known in the West. It is very widely used in Japanese cooking, both fresh and dried (the brownish-black dried Chinese mushrooms are, in fact, shiitake).*

Umeboshi *A salt-dried plum, this is an essential accompaniment to boiled rice for a traditional Japanese breakfast. Fresh plums are soaked in a salty brine, often with red shiso (a Japanese herb also known as beefsteak leaf in the West) and then sun-dried. Umeboshi come in various sizes—from that of a pea to a golfball—and in various shades of red.*

Seaweeds and sea vegetables

Hijiki *A type of dried seaweed, this is normally about ¾ inch long and matchstick-thin. As it remains an intense black, it is often used for its color.*

Kanten *A dried seaweed extract (also called* agar-agar*), this is mainly used to set desserts, in the same way as gelatin.*

Konbu *This is dried kelp, a giant, dark green seaweed. Full of vitamins and minerals, it is often simmered with vegetables, and is an essential ingredient in dashi—the stock that forms the basis of countless Japanese dishes.*

Nori *A paper-thin, dried laver seaweed, this is best known for its use in rolled sushi. A nori sheet comes in the standard size of about 8 by 7 inches. It is often lightly toasted for 2–3 seconds before use, by holding the sheet 2 inches above a gentle heat.*

Wakame *Young seaweed with a delicate flavor and pleasant chewy texture, this is normally available dried, cut into pieces. Wakame is full of vitamin C and minerals, and is used for soup and in salads.*

Tofu *Also called beancurd, this is made from yellow soybeans and is a low-fat source of protein. In Japan, tofu shops still make the curd every day. There are two kinds, soft and firm. Firm tofu is the one most easily obtainable in the West, generally sold packaged in water or vacuum-packed. As it holds together better when cooked, it is recommended for cooking and is used in all the recipes in this book. Fried thin tofu, abura-age, is available fresh or frozen at Japanese food stores. Kinako is ground soybean, mainly used for Japanese cake covering. Freeze-dried tofu, Koya-dofu, was first made by Buddhist monks. After soaking in water it has a rather spongy texture.*

Rice

Glutinous rice (mochi-gome) *Japanese* mochi-gome *is a short-grain, sticky rice, mainly used to make* mochi *(rice cake). Long-grain glutinous rice from other countries can be substituted.*

Japanese rice (kome *or, more politely,* o'kome) *This is a short-grain and slightly sticky variety. Japanese-style rice varies in hardness. Some good brands are, in order of hardness: Kaho-mai, Nishiki, Maruyu, Kokuho (all Californian) and Minori (Spanish).*

Rice cake (mochi) *Made from pounded steamed or boiled glutinous rice. Ready-to-use* mochi *is obtainable in frozen or vacuum packs.*

Noodles

Ramen *Using Chinese-style egg noodles as a guide, the Japanese made their own version, and went on to create not only* shoyu- *but also* miso- *and* dashi-*flavored ramen soups. It is now probably the most popular food in Japan.*

Soba *These fine noodles are made from buckwheat flour. They are usually speckled light brown in color, but may also be pale green (cha-soba) when tea leaves are added. Dried soba is now obtainable from many supermarkets.*

Somen *Very fine white noodles made from wheat flour, somen is eaten cold, dipped in sauce. Asian markets and health-food stores stock dried somen.*

Udon *Another wheat-flour noodle, these are thick and white. They can be bought fresh, frozen, or dried.*

Sauces and seasonings

Mirin *Very thick and sweet rice wine, this is an essential flavoring in Japanese cooking (it is never drunk).* Mirin *gives a very subtle sweet flavor. If it is not available, you can substitute sweet sherry, or sake with a little sugar.*

Miso *A salty paste with a distinctive flavor, made from fermented soybeans, miso is used in soups and salad dressings, and for marinades. There are many types, varying in color, texture, and taste.*

Rice vinegar (su) *Japanese rice vinegar is less acidic than Western wine vinegars. It is essential for making proper* sushi *rice.*

Sake *A fine distilled rice spirit normally drunk lukewarm, sake is an important ingredient in cooking.*

Shochu *A distilled wine made from sake lees, mirin lees, or rice, barley, millet, molasses, and sweet potato.*

Shoyu *The Japanese name for soy sauce, this the most important ingredient in Japanese cooking. Shoyu is made from soybeans, flour, and water, fermented and matured for several months, then pressed to yield the sauce.*

Flavorings

Dashi granules or powder *Japanese fish stock made from* konbu *and* kezuribushi, *or* niboshi *(dried small fish). Nowadays, freeze-dried granules or powder are often used.*

Ginger (shoga) *Fresh ginger is widely used in Japanese cooking. Always peeled and grated, it is often just the juice that is used. Ginger is also pickled, as the sliced root or the young shoots.*

Kezuribushi *Also called* katsuo-bushi *or* hanakatsuo, *these are dried bonito flakes, used to make* dashi *and as a condiment.*

Sansho *A delicately pungent green Japanese pepper, this is ground from the seeds of the prickly ash. Sansho is not used in cooking, but is instead served as a condiment on the table.*

Wasabi *A hot green Japanese horseradish, mainly used with raw fish for sashimi. It is available as a powder or paste. Powdered* wasabi *can be made into a paste by mixing with warm water.*

Ingredients illustrated on previous pages
Top row (*left to right*) shochu; nori sheet, hijiki, kanten, wakame, *and* konbu; *kabocha squash and* satoimo; *pickled ginger;* mirin; umeboshi.
Middle row (*left to right*) glutinous rice *(top),* mochi *(bottom) and Japanese rice;* wasabi; rice vinegar; somen, udon, ramen, *and* soba; tofu, koya-dofu, *and* abura-age; sansho.
Bottom row (*left to right*) kezuribushi *(top and bottom right) and* dashi *(bottom left);* sake; shiitake, daikon, dried shiitake, *and pickled* daikon *(takuan);* shoyu; miso; *cooked adzuki beans (top and bottom), red bean paste, and dried adzuki beans.*

The Japanese kitchen

In line with the increasingly Western look of Japanese homes, the typical Japanese kitchen is also changing rapidly—though only on the surface. It may now have a microwave oven and a food processor, but inside the cabinets there will always be a *daikon-oroshi* (grater), *suribachi* and *surikogi* (mortar and pestle), *makisu* (bamboo mat for rolling *sushi*), *handai* (*sushi* tub), *zaru* (bamboo basket for draining), and an assortment of various sizes of cooking *hashi* (chopsticks).

These very traditional cooking utensils are considered essential to prepare all sorts of food, not just Japanese dishes. Even collectors of every new electric gadget are now finding that the older manual tools are more convenient, simply because they do not require setting up and dismantling, and the tedious cleaning after use. Also, traditional utensils very efficiently do the jobs for which they were specifically designed.

For example, Japanese cooking uses a lot of grated *daikon* and fresh ginger, and both the grated flesh and the juice that is exuded during grating are used in recipes. With ginger, sometimes only the juice is needed. So the *daikon-oroshi* has a small curved base at the end of the spikes to capture the juice. The *suribachi* is made of terracotta in the shape of a pudding bowl, with numerous sharp ridges on the inside surface so that ingredients as diverse as sesame seeds and ground meat or fish can be squashed with the wooden *surikogi* into a paste. A food processor could be used for some of these jobs, but not for small ingredients such as sesame seeds.

The *makisu* is a vital tool for rolling *norimaki* (*nori*-rolled *sushi*), and is also used for rolling other things. The vinegared rice for *sushi* is traditionally mixed in a shallow wooden tub called a *handai*. This works better than a glass or china bowl because wood takes excess moisture from the rice, preventing it from being too sticky. Cooking *hashi* are made of wood because of its gentler touch on ingredients. *Hashi* vary in length from about 10 inches to 20 inches, the longest ones being used for frying.

The Japanese used to cook rice outside the kitchen, using wood as fuel. Every household once had a deep, wooden, barrel-like container with a lid to which freshly cooked rice was transferred and then served from. Sadly, this has now been replaced by the electric rice cooker, which can keep the rice warm all day. Some people still nostalgically remember how delicious rice cooked with wood used to be, and every electrical appliance manufacturer's ultimate aim is to produce a rice cooker that can impart the subtle taste of a wood fire to cooked rice. The electric bread-maker is another recent addition to Japanese kitchens.

Among all the utensils in the Japanese kitchen, the most vital are without doubt a cutting board and a selection of good sharp knives. As Japanese dishes require the minimum of cooking, to preserve the natural textures and flavors of the ingredients, cutting is inevitably the most important and time-consuming part of the preparation. A large, thick wooden cutting board is a cook's dancing stage—the Japanese word for a professional chef, *itamae,* literally means "before the board"—and knives are the essence of the cook. (The Japanese say that if you look into the drawer where the knives are kept, you will discover the cook's heart and soul.)

A set of Japanese knives is not so very different from a Western set, except for the addition of a *sashimi* knife. This is about 12 inches long with a 1 inch wide blade. All Japanese knives have thinner blades than their Western equivalent, except the carver. It is important that knives are kept sharp, and there are special stores to do this, or you can do it yourself using a sharpening stone.

The Japanese often cook at the table, preparing and eating such dishes as *Sukiyaki*, *Shabushabu*, *Oden*, and numerous other hotpots. *Teppanyaki*, or griddle, is also normally cooked at the table. Each household has at least a *sukiyaki* pan, an earthenware pan for other hotpots, and a griddle. Some have a fire ring fixed in the center of the table, while others use a portable gas cooker. Though not essential, these are convenient utensils.

Since foreign cooking—Chinese, Italian, and Indian in particular— is part of the daily diet in modern Japan, in addition to traditional pans, such as a saucepan with a wooden *otoshibuta* (drop-lid) and a square *tamagoyaki* (omelet) pan, most Japanese kitchens will be equipped with one or two woks with bamboo steamer and a set of sauté pans. There is also likely to be a Western dinner set—complete with all tableware and flatware—and sometimes a Chinese one, too.

Cooking Japanese rice
Wash the rice thoroughly, changing the water a few times, until it appears clear, then drain and leave for 1 hour. (If you do not have enough time, soak the rice for 10 minutes, then drain well.) Put the rice in a deep saucepan and add 15 percent more cold water than rice, or 20 percent more water if you have only soaked the rice for 10 minutes. Cover, place on high heat, and bring to a boil. Lower the heat and simmer for 7–13 minutes, or until all the water has been absorbed. Remove from the heat and leave, still covered, for about 10 minutes before serving.

Making *sumeshi* (vinegared rice)
For every 1 cup rice to be boiled, put 2¼ tablespoons rice vinegar or white wine vinegar, ½ tablespoon sugar, and ½ teaspoon sea salt in a measuring cup and stir until dissolved. Cook the rice, then transfer to a *handai* or large mixing bowl and pour the vinegar mixture over. Using a wooden spatula, fold the vinegar into the rice; do not stir. Leave to cool to body temperature before using for *sushi*.

Below *Tricolor Nori-Rolled* Sushi *(page 22)*

SOUPS
AND APPETIZERS

Kenchin Soup with Pork and Vegetables

Kenchin-jiru

Kenchin is a dish of tofu fried with various vegetables, such as carrot, eggplant, gobo *(burdock), and* satoimo *(eddo or taro root). This soup version is made without frying the ingredients, and is a very good family dish for winter. Any firm vegetables can be used instead of those suggested here.* **Serves 4–6**

1 Bring 2¼ cups of water to a boil in a large saucepan. Add the turnips and carrot and cook over high heat for 5 minutes, or until just cooked but still a little hard in the center.

2 Meanwhile, cut the potatoes, *konnyaku*, if used, and tofu into pieces the same size as the turnips and carrot. Slice the pork as thinly as you can, then cut into roughly 1-inch squares.

3 Add the potatoes, *konnyaku*, and pork to the pan. Bring back to a boil and simmer on medium heat for about 3 minutes.

4 Add the chicken bouillon cube and stir gently until the cube dissolves.

5 Dilute the *miso* with a few tablespoons of the soup, then pour into the pan and stir. Check the seasoning. If it's too weak, add more *miso*, a little at a time; if it's too salty, add a little water.

6 Add the tofu pieces and simmer for a further 3 minutes (do not allow to boil). Serve in large, individual soup bowls sprinkled with the scallion and a little chili powder.

1–2 turnips *cut into bite-sized pieces*

1 carrot *cut into bite-sized pieces*

1–2 potatoes

½ x 8-ounce cake *konnyaku* (optional)

½ x 10-ounce cake firm tofu

8 ounces boneless pork

1 chicken bouillon cube

1½ ounces *miso* (about 3 tablespoons)

To serve:

1 scallion *minced*

hot chili powder

Miso Soup with Tofu and Snow Peas

Tofu no Misoshiru

An authentic Japanese breakfast always starts by sipping misoshiru, *which is fish stock soup mixed with* miso. *The added ingredients, which change daily, are normally vegetables or small shellfish. Tofu is very commonly used, along with green vegetables such as* wakame, *spinach, and snow peas, or* nameko *mushrooms—tiny, pea-like mushrooms that are only available cooked in cans.* **Serves 4**

12–20 snow peas

1½ ounces *miso* (about 3 tablespoons)

½ x 10-ounce cake firm tofu *finely diced*

1 teaspoon *dashi* granules

1 scallion *minced*

1 If the snow peas are large, cut them in half crosswise, slightly on a diagonal. Put the *miso* in a small cup or bowl and mix in a few tablespoons of water to dilute the *miso*.

2 Bring 2½ cups of water to a boil in a saucepan. Add the snow peas and boil for 1 minute. Lower the heat, and stir in the diluted *miso*. Then add the diced tofu. Bring almost to a boil again, and add the *dashi* granules, stirring. Immediately remove from the heat (do not allow to boil) and add the scallion.

3 Serve hot in individual soup bowls.

Dashi

To make authentic dashi *without the convenience of granules, place a 4-inch sheet of* konbu *in a saucepan with 2 quarts of water and cook on medium heat for about 10 minutes, or until the* konbu *fully expands; do not boil. Add 1 ounce* kezuribushi *and simmer for a further 5 minutes. Remove from the heat and leave until the* kezuribushi *settles on the bottom of the pan, then strain, discarding the* kezuribushi *and* konbu. Dashi *can be frozen for up to 3 months.* **Makes about 2 quarts**

Thick Egg Soup

Chawanmushi

This steamed soup is very nutritious and filling, and, being soft and easily digested, is particularly good when you do not have much appetite. Traditional ingredients are seafood and chicken coupled with vegetables, but you can also use sausage, ham, or even bacon. Plain Chawanmushi—stock and eggs without additional ingredients—is also delicious and very good for infants. **Serves 4**

1 Thinly slice the chicken into bite-sized pieces, cutting on a diagonal. Sprinkle with a little *sake* and *shoyu*. Slice each mushroom into 4, cutting diagonally to make slices of even thickness. If the snow peas are large, cut them in half crosswise, slightly on a diagonal. Divide these ingredients equally among 4 soup bowls or cups.

2 Warm the stock and season with the salt, *mirin*, and 1 tablespoon of *shoyu*. Leave to cool, then gradually pour into the beaten eggs, stirring gently all the time. (It should not form bubbles or foam.)

3 Pour the egg mixture over the ingredients in each of the bowls or cups. Cover with foil and set in the top of a steamer. Steam, covered, over low heat for 25–30 minutes, or until set. Alternatively, place in a shallow baking dish half-filled with hot water and cook in a preheated oven at 425°F for 25–30 minutes. You can also place the bowls or cups in a deep saucepan one-third-filled with boiling water and cook over low heat for 20 minutes. Check constantly after 15 minutes to be sure the custard does not overcook.

4 Serve immediately, garnished with chopped cilantro or parsley.

2½–3 ounces skinless, boneless chicken breast

sake

shoyu

4 fresh shiitake or button mushrooms *stems trimmed*

4 snow peas

2 cups chicken stock

½ teaspoon sea salt

1 tablespoon *mirin* or ½ tablespoon sugar

3 eggs *beaten*

To serve:

fresh cilantro or parsley *minced*

Clear Soup with Mussels and Watercress

Sumashi-jiru

This refreshing soup consists of a simple fish stock flavored with a little shoyu *and a mixture of added ingredients. Popular additions are tofu, shellfish, or chicken paired with a green vegetable, such as* wakame, *spinach, snow peas, and green beans, or with a white vegetable, such as bean sprouts and* hakusai. *Fine* somen *also make a decorative addition. Use authentic* dashi *(see page 18) instead of* dashi *granules and water, if you like.* **Serves 4**

1 ounce dried *somen*

16–20 mussels (about 1 pound) *cleaned*

1½ tablespoons *shoyu*

½ tablespoon *mirin*

1 teaspoon *dashi* granules

sea salt

4 sprigs of watercress

finely grated or shredded zest and juice of ½ lime

1 Cook the *somen* following the package directions, then drain and rinse well under cold running water. Drain and keep aside.

2 Bring 2½ cups of water to a boil in a saucepan. Add the mussels and cook briskly over high heat until all of the mussels are open (discard any that remain stubbornly closed, as they are dead). Lower the heat and add the *shoyu*, *mirin*, and *dashi* granules. Stir to mix. Check the seasoning, adding a pinch of salt if necessary.

3 Add the watercress. Turn up the heat again and, just before the liquid boils, remove from the heat.

4 Divide the cooked *somen* equally among 4 individual soup bowls. Into each put 4 or 5 mussels and a sprig of watercress, then pour the soup over. Sprinkle each serving with a little lime zest and a squeeze of lime juice. Serve hot.

Tricolor Nori-Rolled Sushi

Hosomaki-zushi

The term sushi *is a corruption of* sumeshi, *meaning vinegared rice, which is a major component of all* sushi *dishes. There are roughly four types of* sushi: nigiri *(hand-molded, with a piece of raw fish on top),* maki-zushi *(nori rolls),* oshi-zushi *(pressed), and* chirashi *(mixed). This pretty, thin roll is the easiest type of* sushi *to make and is good for parties. You need a* makisu *(small bamboo mat) or similarly flexible tablemat for rolling.*

Makes 36 pieces

1–2 teaspoons *wasabi* powder or paste or horseradish relish

3 sheets of dried *nori*

a 2½-inch piece of cucumber *quartered lengthwise, seeded, and cut into ¼ inch thick strips*

4 ounces smoked salmon *cut into ¼ inch thick strips*

3 crab sticks *halved lengthwise and half of the white part discarded*

For the *sumeshi* (vinegared rice):

1½ cups Japanese rice

5 tablespoons rice vinegar or white wine vinegar

1½ tablespoons sugar

1½ teaspoons sea salt

To serve:

shoyu

1 First make the *sumeshi* (see page 13). Leave to cool while you prepare the remaining ingredients.

2 If using powdered *wasabi*, dissolve it in 1–2 teaspoons of water, stirring well to make a soft, but not runny, claylike paste.

3 Place the *makisu* on the work surface so you can roll the mat away from yourself. Cut the *nori* sheets crosswise in half and place one piece horizontally on the *makisu*. Using your hands, spread about 3–4 tablespoons of *sumeshi* on the *nori*, leaving about a ½-inch margin clear on the long side furthest from you. Spread a tiny bit of *wasabi* across the rice in the center, slightly nearer to you, then place a line of cucumber strips on it, arranging them end to end. Roll up the *makisu*, to wrap the cucumber in the center of the rice, gently pressing into a log shape. Make sure the long sides of the *nori* overlap. Remove the *sushi* roll from the *makisu*. Repeat with the remaining cucumber and then the smoked salmon and crab sticks, making 2 rolls for each ingredient.

4 Cut each roll across into 6 pieces. Serve with a little *shoyu* in individual tiny dishes, for dipping.

Squid Sushi

Ika-zushi

Squid is one of the most commonly used seafoods in Japan, both at home and in restaurants. It is eaten raw, as sashimi, *as well as cooked. One of the most popular ways of cooking it is stuffed—the ginger-flavored rice stuffing here is particularly delicious.* **Serves 4–6**

1 Skin each squid by holding the two flaps together with one hand and pulling them down and off the squid body. Discard the skin from the flaps.

2 Mix together the *sake*, *shoyu*, and sugar in a large shallow saucepan and bring to a boil on high heat, stirring constantly to dissolve the sugar. Lower the heat to medium, and add the squid bodies, flaps, and tentacles. Cook for 2–3 minutes, turning the pieces so that they take on color evenly. Remove from the heat and leave to cool in the liquid.

3 Make the *sumeshi* (see page 13). Leave to cool.

4 Mince half of the pickled ginger. Chop the cooked squid tentacles and flaps. Using a wooden spatula, fold the minced pickled ginger and chopped squid tentacles and flaps into the *sumeshi*. Do not mash the rice.

5 Stuff the squid bodies tightly with the *sumeshi* mixture. Cut each stuffed squid crosswise into ½ inch thick slices, then halve each slice. Arrange on a bed of bamboo or other green leaves on a platter and garnish with the remaining pickled ginger.

2 medium squid (2 pounds) *cleaned*

3 tablespoons *sake*

3 tablespoons *shoyu*

2 tablespoons sugar

3 ounces Pickled Ginger (see page 104) or 1 x 3-ounce package pickled ginger *drained*

For the *sumeshi* (vinegared rice):

1 cup Japanese rice

2 tablespoons rice vinegar or white wine vinegar

½ tablespoon sugar

½ teaspoon sea salt

To serve:

bamboo or green leaves

Mackerel Sushi

Saba-zushi

This dish makes a terrific appetizer, and is easily prepared at home. **Makes 16 pieces**

1 fresh mackerel (about 1 pound)
filleted and trimmed

sea salt

rice vinegar

For the *sumeshi* (vinegared rice):

1 cup Japanese rice

**2½ tablespoons rice vinegar or
white wine vinegar**

½ tablespoon sugar

½ teaspoon sea salt

To serve:

lemon wedges

cress or watercress

shoyu

1 Sprinkle a layer of salt over the bottom of a dish and put the mackerel fillets on top. Cover the mackerel fillets completely with salt. Leave for 3–4 hours (or overnight) in the refrigerator.

2 Make the *sumeshi* (see page 13), using slightly more vinegar than usual, and leave to cool.

3 Rinse the mackerel under cold running water to wash off the salt. Pat dry. Remove any remaining bones with tweezers. Place the fillets on a plate and sprinkle with vinegar on both sides. Leave for 15 minutes. Using your fingers, remove the transparent skin from the mackerel fillets, working from head to tail, leaving the silver pattern on the flesh intact.

4 Place a sheet of plastic wrap, about 10 inches square, on a *makisu* or flexible tablemat. Put a mackerel fillet on the wrap, skin side down. Using your hands, shape half the *sumeshi* into a stick. Place the stick on the mackerel fillet and spread out evenly to the length of the fillet. Wrap the plastic wrap around the mackerel and rice, enclosing the ends.

5 Roll up in the *makisu*, gently pressing into an even shape, finishing with the mackerel fillet on top of the rice. Remove the plastic-wrapped *sushi* from the *makisu*. Repeat for the other fillet. Leave in a cool place for a few hours. (Never refrigerate.)

6 Unwrap the *sushi* and place rice side down on a cutting board. Cut into ¾–1¼ inch thick slices. Serve garnished with lemon wedges and cress, and accompany with a little *shoyu*.

Egg-Cup Sushi

Kodemari-zushi

Sushi is, without doubt, the most popular of all Japanese "fast" foods. Here is a version that can easily be made at home. **Makes 24 pieces**

1 Make the *sumeshi* (see page 13). Leave to cool.

2 Season the beaten eggs with a little salt. Cook in a lightly oiled saucepan until softly scrambled. Leave to cool. Meanwhile, place the anchovy fillets in between paper towels and pat off the excess oil. Mince the anchovies to make an almost pastelike consistency. Using a wooden spatula, fold into the *sumeshi*. Do not mash the rice.

3 Line an egg cup with plastic wrap measuring about 8 inches square; the plastic should hang over the rim of the cup. Line the cup with a piece of smoked salmon, filling any gaps with small pieces of salmon. Put 1 tablespoonful of the *sumeshi* mixture in the cup and press down gently with your thumbs. Do not over fill. Trim the excess salmon from the rim. Lift up the plastic wrap and turn out the molded *sushi*, upside down, onto a plate. Repeat to make 12 pieces. Garnish each with a caper berry.

4 Lay a new piece of plastic wrap in the egg cup. Place about 1 teaspoonful of the scrambled eggs on the bottom. Gently press to make a firm base— the egg should come about halfway up the side of the cup. Place about 1 tablespoonful of the *sumeshi* mixture on the egg and again gently press down with your thumbs. Do not over fill. Using the plastic wrap, turn out the molded *sushi*, upside down, onto a plate. Repeat this process for the remainder of the rice and egg. It should make about 12 pieces.

5 Arrange all the molded *sushi* on a large serving plate, garnish with lemon wedges and watercress, and serve.

2 eggs *beaten*

sea salt

1 x 2-ounce can anchovy fillets *drained*

6 smoked salmon slices (about 5 ounces) *halved*

12 caper berries

For the *sumeshi* (vinegared rice):

1 cup Japanese rice

2 tablespoons rice vinegar or white wine vinegar

½ tablespoon sugar

½ teaspoon sea salt

To serve:

lemon wedges

watercress

Grilled Tofu, Eggplant, and Potato with Miso Paste

Dengaku

The name of this street food no doubt derives from the dengaku *dancers that toured villages to entertain farmers. This dish can be served as an appetizer or snack. The sweet* miso *paste can be applied to almost any vegetable after grilling.* **Serves 4–8**

1 First press the tofu. Put the cake of firm tofu on a cutting board and place at an angle over the sink, so that liquid from the tofu runs off. Set another board or a flat plate on top of the tofu and place a weight such as a heavy book on top to press the tofu and squeeze out excess liquid. Leave for about 30 minutes. Cut the tofu into 8 pieces, each ½ inch thick. Thread lengthwise onto metal skewers, 2 pieces on each skewer.

2 Cook the potato in boiling water until almost tender but still very firm; drain. Cut into eight 1- by 2-inch pieces that are ½ inch thick. Cut the eggplant into 8 similar-size pieces. Thread the potato and eggplant pieces lengthwise onto metal skewers, 2 pieces on each skewer.

3 Put the *miso* in a small saucepan and stir in the *sake* and sugar. Place the pan on low heat and, stirring all the time, gradually add 3 tablespoons of water. Keep stirring until the sauce becomes thick but not too hard. Add the lime juice, then immediately remove from the heat. Leave to cool to room temperature. (The *dengaku miso* keeps well in the refrigerator.)

4 Grill the tofu, potato, and eggplant over a charcoal fire, or under the broiler, for 2–3 minutes, until lightly browned on each side and heated through. Remove from the heat and thickly spread one side with the *dengaku miso*. Sprinkle toasted sesame seeds over. Remove from the skewers and serve hot on a bed of leaves.

1 x 10-ounce cake firm tofu

1 potato

1 eggplant

toasted sesame seeds

For the *dengaku miso* paste:

3 ounces *miso* (about 6 tablespoons)

3 tablespoons *sake*

3 tablespoons sugar

juice of ¼ lime

To serve:

green leaves, such as bamboo

Fried Tofu Balls

Ganmodoki

Ganmodoki *is readily available at tofu shops in Japan, where it is normally cooked with other vegetables or meat. This homemade version is a little different from the ready-made one, and is so much nicer, as you can eat it fresh and hot, all on its own.* **Serves 4**

1 x 10-ounce cake firm tofu

a 1- by 2-inch piece of *konbu*

2 fresh or dried shiitake mushrooms *stems trimmed*

¼ carrot

8 green beans

1 egg

pinch of sea salt

dash each of *shoyu* and *mirin*

1 tablespoon black sesame seeds

vegetable oil for deep-frying

To serve:

lemon wedges

1 Press the tofu (see page 29).

2 Meanwhile, soak the *konbu* in water for 10 minutes, or until fully expanded; drain. If using dried shiitake, soak in warm water for at least 30 minutes, then drain.

3 Cut the carrot, beans, *konbu*, and mushrooms into ¼-inch shreds.

4 Put the tofu in a food processor with the egg, salt, *shoyu*, and *mirin*. Process to a very smooth consistency, then transfer to a mixing bowl. Add all the vegetable shreds and the sesame seeds and mix well.

5 Heat oil for deep-frying in a frying pan to 237°F. Spoon 1 heaped tablespoonful of the tofu mixture onto your wet palm and shape into a small oval about ½ inch thick. Put into the hot oil and deep-fry for 2–3 minutes or until both sides are a light golden color; drain on paper towels. Repeat this process until all the mixture is used up. There should be about 12 balls.

6 When all the tofu balls have been fried, heat up the oil again to 300°F. Fry the balls again briefly to make them crisp. Serve hot in 4 individual plates garnished with lemon wedges.

Pan-Fried Koya-dofu

Yaki Koya-dofu

Koya-dofu is a freeze-dried tofu, originating out of a Buddhist monastery on the Koya mountain—monks used to leave tofu cubes outside in cold weather to freeze and dry so that it would keep. Nowadays it's all done by a freezer and dryer at factories. Like all tofu, Koya-dofu is very nutritious but rather bland, so it is always cooked in a flavoured liquid, often with vegetables, fish, or meat. **Serves 4**

1 Soak the *Koya-dofu* in hot water (about 120°F) for 10 minutes, or until fully expanded. Drain and squeeze out as much water as possible. Slice each cake horizontally in half, then cut each slice into 4 triangles.

2 Heat 1 cup water in a saucepan and add the *dashi*, *shoyu*, *mirin*, and salt. Add the *Koya-dofu* triangles and simmer for about 5 minutes. Remove from the heat and set aside.

3 Mix the egg yolks with the parsley in a small bowl.

4 Heat a frying pan on high, then add the oil. One piece at a time, roughly squeeze the flavored liquid out of the *Koya-dofu* and dip into the egg yolk mixture. Pan-fry, a few pieces at a time, until both sides are golden brown. Serve hot.

2 cakes *Koya-dofu* (1¼ ounces in total)

½ teaspoon *dashi* granules

4 tablespoons *shoyu*

2 tablespoons *mirin* or 1 tablespoon sugar

¼ teaspoon sea salt

3 egg yolks *beaten*

2–3 sprigs of parsley *chopped*

2–3 tablespoons vegetable oil

Sardines Marinated in Vinegar and Chili

Iwashi no Nanban-zuke

Nanban *means "southern barbarians"—a title seventeenth-century Japan gave to South-east Asian countries such as Singapore and Indonesia, and, in a broader sense, to all European-influenced things arriving in Japan through these countries. The name accounts for the rather un-Japanese way of cooking fish in this recipe: by frying and then marinating in vinegary* shoyu. *This popular dish is served as an hors d' oeuvre in most Japanese restaurants and snack bars.* **Serves 4**

vegetable oil for deep-frying

8–12 small sardines (about 1½ pounds) *cleaned*

all-purpose flour

1 onion *halved and thinly sliced*

For the *nanban* sauce:

7 tablespoons rice vinegar

5 tablespoons *mirin*

½ teaspoon *dashi* **granules**

3 tablespoons sugar

2 tablespoons *shoyu*

½ teaspoon sea salt

2 fresh hot red chili peppers *seeded and thinly sliced*

1 Heat oil for deep-frying to 340°F. Dust the sardines with flour and deep-fry, 3 or 4 at a time, in the hot oil for 2–3 minutes on each side or until golden brown. Remove from the oil and drain on paper towels.

2 Mix all the ingredients for the *nanban* sauce in a saucepan with 5 tablespoons water. Bring to a boil. Add the onion slices and remove from the heat. Pour into a large bowl.

3 Heat up the oil again until it is about 350°F. Return the sardines to the oil, in batches, and fry to make them really crisp. Remove from the oil and immediately put into the sauce. When all the sardines have been fried a second time, spoon the sauce over them so that all are covered. Leave to marinate overnight in the refrigerator.

4 To serve, remove the sardines from the sauce and arrange on a large serving dish or individual plates. Spoon a little of the sauce over the sardines, if liked. Serve chilled or at room temperature.

Fried Giant Prawns

Ebi Fry

Many different kinds of prawns and shrimp, in varying sizes, are available in Japan—sold fresh, even live—and they are used in many ways. An exceptionally delicious sashimi *is fresh* ama-ebi *(sweet shrimp). This very popular and traditional dish is found on the menu of most Japanese bars, cafés, and restaurants.* **Serves 4**

8 raw king or tiger prawns or jumbo shrimp *(the biggest you can find)*

sea salt

sake **or white wine**

vegetable oil for deep-frying

all-purpose flour

1 extra large egg *lightly beaten*

dry white bread crumbs

To serve:

lemon wedges

powdered *sansho* **(optional)**

1 Peel the prawns, retaining the last tail section, and devein. Make several shallow cuts crosswise under the belly of each prawn to prevent it from curling during cooking. Sprinkle with salt and a little *sake*, and set aside.

2 Heat oil for deep-frying in a wok or deep frying pan to about 325°F.

3 Holding a prawn by the tail, coat it lightly with flour, then dip into the egg and, finally, coat with bread crumbs (do not coat the tail). Deep-fry the prawns, a few at a time, for 1–2 minutes, turning frequently, until golden brown all over. Drain on a wire rack or paper towels.

4 Arrange 2 fried prawns on each of 4 individual plates, placing them on a sheet of folded paper, if preferred. Garnish with lemon wedges and serve immediately, accompanied by salt and *sansho* in separate dishes or jars.

Soft-Cooked Octopus

Tako no Yawaraka-ni

Octopus is frequently cooked on streetside stalls in Japan, either grilled in whole tentacles over a charcoal fire and then dipped in shoyu, or cut into pieces and pan-fried in batter in the shape of a ball (this is called takoyaki*). The* takoyaki-ya *(octopus-ball street vendor) normally has a large pan with pingpong-ball-shaped wells in which the octopus balls are cooked. Octopus is also used raw for* sashimi *and in simmered dishes such as the one here.*

Serves 6–8

1 Rub salt all over the octopus and scrub off the sliminess by hand. Wash under cold running water. Cut each tentacle and body part into bite-sized pieces.

2 Put the chicken stock and *sake* in a saucepan and bring to a boil. Add the octopus and cook on high heat for about 5 minutes or until the octopus is tender.

3 Add the *mirin* and *shoyu*, and simmer, covered, for 10 minutes. Remove from the heat and leave to cool in the liquid until ready to serve.

1 small octopus (14 ounces)
cleaned

sea salt

1¼ cups chicken stock

5 tablespoons *sake*

3 tablespoons *mirin*

3 tablespoons *shoyu*

Sole Sashimi Salad

Hirame no Salada

For sashimi *you must use only the very best part of very fresh fish such as tuna, salmon, sole, sea bass, shrimp, and squid. If you are a little uncomfortable about eating completely raw fish, try this vinegared fish salad first.* **Serves 4–6**

1 If you are filleting and skinning the fish yourself, use a sharp filleting knife to make a slit down the center of the fish on one side, next to the bone, then slide the blade between the flesh and small bones, working from the center out toward the fins to separate the flesh from the bones. Repeat this to take 2 fillets from each side, making 4 fillets in all. To skin them, place one fillet on the cutting board, skin side down, and, holding down the tail end with your finger, run the knife blade at a sharp angle between the flesh and the skin, working from the tail upward. Repeat this with the remaining fillets.

2 Plunge the fillets, one at a time, into boiling water and boil for 30 seconds, then plunge into ice water and immediately drain and pat dry on paper towels. Very thinly slice the fillets crosswise, with the knife blade held at an angle. Place the slices flat on a large plate and sprinkle evenly with the vinegar. Leave for 5 minutes.

3 Meanwhile, put the sesame seeds in a small dry saucepan and toss over high heat until the seeds start popping. Remove from the heat and set aside. Mix together the *shoyu*, lemon juice, *wasabi* paste, and sesame oil.

4 Drain the fish slices and arrange on a bed of mixed salad leaves on a large serving plate or 4 individual plates. Pour the *shoyu* dressing over the fish and sprinkle with the toasted sesame seeds. Serve garnished with lemon wedges.

1 sole (about 1½ pounds) *filleted and skinned*

6 tablespoons rice vinegar or white wine vinegar

1 tablespoon sesame seeds

3 tablespoons *shoyu*

3 tablespoons lemon juice

1–2 teaspoons *wasabi* **paste**

½ tablespoon toasted sesame oil

mixed salad leaves

To serve:

lemon wedges

Grilled Skewered Chicken

Yakitori

This is Japan's most popular street food. You can find yakitori *bars everywhere, be it in the busiest centers of Tokyo or provincial station arcades where businessmen drop in for a drink or two on the way home. Meat from the chicken leg is most commonly used, although other parts of the chicken, even the livers, are also excellent.* Yakitori *can be grilled outdoors over charcoal, and makes very good party fare. If you want to serve it on wooden toothpicks, grill the chicken on metal skewers and then transfer to the toothpicks.* **Serves 4–8**

6–8 chicken thighs (about 1 pound) *skinned and boned*

For the *taré* sauce:

3 tablespoons *sake*

scant 5 tablespoons *shoyu*

1 tablespoon *mirin*

1 tablespoon sugar

To serve:

lemon wedges

powdered *sansho* or hot chili powder (optional)

1 Soak 12–16 bamboo skewers (each about 6 inches long) in water for 30 minutes. Cut the chicken thighs into ¾ inch square pieces (6–8 per thigh). Thread 4 pieces onto each skewer.

2 Combine all the ingredients for the *taré* sauce in a small saucepan and bring to a boil, stirring. Simmer for 5 minutes. Remove from the heat.

3 Grill the skewered chicken over a charcoal fire, or cook under the broiler, until lightly browned all over. Remove from the heat, one at a time, baste with the *taré* sauce, and return to the heat to dry the sauce. Then remove and baste with more sauce. Repeat this process a few more times until all the chicken pieces are golden brown.

4 Serve with lemon wedges and *sansho* or chili powder.

Skewered Chicken Meatballs
Kushizashi Tori Dango

Poultry has played an important part in Japanese cuisine for much longer than red meat, and dishes using ground chicken, such as this one, are the base of much home cooking. This pretty chicken dish is particularly good for parties. It is also a very convenient grill item as its preparation can be done well ahead. **Serves 6–8**

1 Soak 8 bamboo skewers (about 6 inches long) in water for 30 minutes before cooking, or you can grill the chicken balls on metal skewers. Put the ground chicken, egg, sugar, and *shoyu* in a food processor and blend until smooth. Transfer to a mixing bowl. Spoon some of the mixture onto your wet hand and shape into a ball about half the size of a golfball. Repeat this until all the mixture is used up. You will have about 24 balls.

2 Bring a large saucepan of water to a boil and put in the chicken balls. Cook for 7–8 minutes, then drain. (You can prepare up to this stage, then refrigerate the balls.)

3 Mix together the *yuan* sauce ingredients in a small saucepan. Bring to a boil over high heat and reduce the sauce by a third. Remove from the heat and set aside.

4 Thread 3 chicken balls onto each soaked bamboo skewer (or 4–6 balls onto each metal skewer). Grill over a charcoal fire, or cook under the broiler, until both sides are golden brown. Remove from the heat, one skewer at a time, baste the chicken balls with the *yuan* sauce, and return to the heat to dry the sauce. Repeat this process 2 or 3 more times.

5 If you have used metal skewers, transfer the chicken balls to wooden toothpicks, putting 1 or 2 balls on each one. Arrange on a large serving dish and serve with a jar of *sansho*.

9 ounces ground chicken

1 small egg

1 tablespoon sugar

1 tablespoon *shoyu*

For the *yuan* sauce:

6 tablespoons *mirin*

4 tablespoons *shoyu*

3 tablespoons *sake*

To serve:

sansho

MAIN

DISHES

Mackerel Tatsuta Fry

Saba no Tatsuta-age

This dish takes its name from Tatsuta—an area within Nara, the ancient capital of Japan—where the method of marinating and then frying fish is thought to originate. Mackerel is much used in Japanese cooking, particularly at family restaurants and at home, because of its easy availability all year round. When it's really fresh, within hours of the catch, it can be eaten just vinegared, but otherwise it's best when partnered with strong flavors such as ginger and shoyu *and then cooked.* **Serves 4–6**

2 mackerel (2 pounds) *filleted*

5 tablespoons *sake* or white wine

4 tablespoons *shoyu*

a 1¼-inch piece of fresh ginger *peeled and grated*

cornstarch

vegetable oil for deep-frying

To serve:

lettuce leaves

lemon wedges

1 Place each fillet skin side down on a cutting board and slice it crosswise, diagonally along the grain, into ½ inch thick pieces.

2 Mix together the *sake*, *shoyu*, and grated ginger in a shallow dish. Lay the mackerel slices in the dish and turn so that all are coated in the sauce mixture. Leave to marinate for at least 10 minutes. Drain, then toss the mackerel in cornstarch to dust thoroughly.

3 Heat oil in a wok or a deep frying pan to 310°F. Slide the mackerel pieces into the oil, a few at a time, and fry for 2–3 minutes, turning 2 or 3 times, until golden brown all over. Remove from the oil and drain on a wire rack or paper towels.

4 Arrange the fried mackerel on the bed of lettuce leaves on each of 4 individual plates, garnish with lemon wedges, and serve hot.

Fried Flounder

Karei no Kara-age

Although used more widely today, deep-frying is a relatively non-traditional method in otherwise non-fatty Japanese cooking—this dish undoubtedly has a foreign, probably Portuguese, influence. Indeed, the Japanese normally serve fried food with a dashi or daikon sauce for dipping, to make it taste less oily and more refreshing. This popular dish is ideal for making at home. **Serves 4**

1 Cut the fish fillets in half lengthwise to make 4 narrow fillets, then into about 2 inch square pieces. Dredge in cornstarch, shaking off any excess. Set aside.

2 Next make *momiji-oroshi* (grated maple leaf) with the *daikon* and the chilies. Make 4–5 deep holes in the piece of *daikon* by pushing in a *hashi* or a metal kebab skewer from one flat cut side. Push the chili strips into the holes (if the holes are narrow, cut the chili lengthwise to fit). Grate the *daikon* together with the chili. The resulting bright red relish has the color of maple leaves in the fall, hence the name.

3 Heat the oil in a wok or a deep frying pan to about 310°F. Deep-fry the fish pieces for 2–3 minutes or until golden brown all over; drain on a wire rack or paper towels. Heat the oil to 325°F and fry the fish pieces again for 30 seconds to make them crisp. Drain on a wire rack or paper towels.

4 Mix together the lemon juice and *shoyu*, and divide among 4 small individual dishes. Arrange the fried fish, on decorative paper, on 4 individual plates and garnish with lemon or lime wedges. Serve immediately, accompanied by the dipping sauce and the *momiji-oroshi* in a small bowl. Diners mix the *momiji-oroshi* with their portion of sauce, dip in the fish, and eat.

2 large flounder or sole fillets with skin (1 pound)

cornstarch

vegetable oil for deep-frying

For the *momiji-oroshi*:

a 4-inch piece of *daikon* (9 ounces) *peeled*

1–2 fresh hot red chili peppers

For the dipping sauce:

juice of ½ lemon

1½ tablespoons *shoyu*

To serve:

lemon or lime wedges

Seared Yuan Salmon

Sake no Yuan-yaki

Yuan sauce is a simple mixture of mirin, shoyu, and sake. *It gives a subtle flavor to rather bland ingredients such as white fish and chicken, and enhances the flavors of fish such as salmon.* **Serves 4**

4 pieces of salmon fillet with skin (about 1⅔ pounds) *scaled if necessary*

sea salt

9 ounces okra

vegetable oil

For the *yuan* sauce:

5 tablespoons *mirin*

3 tablespoons *shoyu*

2 tablespoons *sake*

juice of ½ lime

To serve:

½ lime *thinly sliced*

1 Pat the pieces of salmon dry with paper towels, then sprinkle each with a pinch of salt.

2 Make the *yuan* sauce in a shallow dish by mixing together the *mirin, shoyu, sake,* and lime juice. Lay the pieces of salmon in the dish, skin side up, and leave to marinate for at least 15 minutes.

3 Cook the okra in lightly salted boiling water for 1–2 minutes or until just tender but still crunchy. Drain and immediately put under cold running water to prevent further cooking and to set the green color. Cut off the hard stem part.

4 Heat a frying pan or a ridged cast-iron grill pan with a little oil. Put the salmon fillets in the pan, skin side up, and cook over medium heat for 2–3 minutes, or until golden brown, then turn the salmon pieces and sear the other sides. Alternatively, grill the salmon: Thread 3 long stainless-steel skewers horizontally through each piece of salmon in a fan shape so that you can handle the 3 skewers in one hand. Grill, skin side down, over a medium charcoal fire for 2 minutes, or until golden brown, then turn and cook the meat side for 1–2 minutes.

5 Arrange a seared piece of salmon on each of 4 individual plates, garnish with the lime slices and cooked okra, and serve immediately.

Swordfish Tataki

Kajiki-maguro no Tataki

Tataki is a casual form of sashimi. *Originally it was made from minced fresh fish, but now the fish may be parboiled or lightly grilled. Many of the regional coastal towns in Japan have their own* tataki *specialties, and it's a real treat to taste the very best fish at the right place in the right season. This lightly boiled swordfish is easy to prepare and very delicious.*
Serves 4

a 14-ounce swordfish steak

sea salt

a 4-inch piece of large *daikon* (9 ounces) *peeled and grated*

10–15 stalks of fresh chive or 1–2 scallions *minced*

1 tablespoon chopped fresh ginger

1 teaspoon chopped garlic

1 fresh hot red chili pepper *seeded and minced*

For the citrus sauce:

2 tablespoons lime juice

2 tablespoons *shoyu*

2 tablespoons *sake*

To serve:

lime wedges

1 Thinly slice the swordfish into 1- by 2-inch pieces. Plunge, a few at a time, into a pan of lightly salted boiling water. Boil for 30 seconds or until lightly cooked through, then drain and immediately put into ice water. Drain and pat dry with paper towels.

2 Arrange the fish on a large serving plate or 4 individual plates and put the grated *daikon*, chives, ginger, garlic, and chili on top. Garnish with lime wedges.

3 Mix together the lime juice, *shoyu*, and *sake*, and divide among 4 small individual dishes. Serve the fish with the citrus sauce.

Assorted Tempura

Tempura Moriawase

Tempura is an extremely versatile dish, as it can be made with a variety of ingredients and can be presented in many ways, but it is usually served with daikon. For an all-vegetable tempura (Kakiage), shred 1 carrot and 1 parsnip and cut some green beans into a similar size. Put all the vegetables in the batter, then deep-fry a spoonful at a time. **Serves 4**

1 Peel the prawns, retaining the last tail section, and devein. Make a few slits along the belly to prevent the prawns from curling during cooking.

2 Cut the fish fillets into pieces about 2 inches long, and roll in flour. Heat oil for deep-frying to about 340°F. Meanwhile, cook the snow peas in boiling water for 2 minutes, then drain and rinse with cold running water. Set aside.

3 When the oil is almost hot enough, make the batter: Lightly mix the egg yolk with 7 fluid ounces ice water, then add all the flour at once. Using *hashi* (chopsticks) or a fork, very lightly fold the flour into the liquid with only 4–5 strokes. The batter should be just loosely combined and still very lumpy.

4 Dip the mushrooms in the batter and deep-fry for 1–3 minutes or until golden yellow; drain on a rack. Next deep-fry the prawns (dipping them into the batter one at a time, holding the tail) and then the fish fillets. When all the ingredients have been deep-fried, arrange a quarter of each with the snow peas, on decorative paper, on individual plates.

5 Just before the deep-frying is completed, bring 7 fluid ounces water to a boil in a saucepan and add the *dashi* granules, *mirin*, and *shoyu*. Pour into individual dipping bowls and serve garnished with grated *daikon* and ginger.

4 raw king prawns or 8 raw large shrimp

4 flounder or sole fillets

all-purpose flour

vegetable oil for deep-frying

8 snow peas

4–8 fresh shiitake mushrooms or button mushrooms *stems trimmed then cut in half if large*

For the batter:

1 egg yolk *beaten*

1⅓ cups all-purpose flour *sifted*

For the dipping sauce:

½ teaspoon *dashi* granules

4 tablespoons *mirin*

5 tablespoons *shoyu*

To serve:

½ medium *daikon* (about 8 ounces) *peeled and grated*

a 2-inch piece of fresh ginger *peeled and grated*

47

Seafood Griddle

Teppan-yaki

Cooking at the table is very popular in Japan, and most homes have a portable electric griddle. It's fun and very easy—all you need to do is cut the ingredients into bite-sized pieces and then let everybody cook their own dinner. Here, squid and prawns are used, but scallops, salmon, monkfish, or cod steak are all suitable. **Serves 4–6**

1 Skin the squid by holding the two flaps together with one hand and pulling them down and off the squid body. Discard the skin from the flaps. Cut the skinned squid body in half lengthwise and make fine cuts in a cross-hatch pattern on the skinned side, to prevent the squid from curling during cooking. Separate the tentacles, and cut the body and flaps into 1½- by 1-inch pieces. Arrange all the pieces decoratively on a platter with the king prawns.

2 Arrange all the vegetables on another platter.

3 Place a lightly oiled griddle or hot plate in the center of the dining table set with small individual dishes. Serve the seafood and vegetable platters on the table, together with the grated *daikon*, minced scallions and chili, lemon wedges, and *shoyu* in separate plates or bowls. Diners mix their own sauce, and fry the seafood and vegetables for themselves.

1 small squid (9 ounces) *cleaned*

12 raw king prawns *peeled*

1 small eggplant *cut in half lengthwise and then into ½ inch thick half-moons*

1 zucchini *cut into ½ inch thick rounds*

5 ounces fresh shiitake or button mushrooms *stems trimmed and then cut in half if large*

2 cups bean sprouts

To serve:

a 4-inch piece of large daikon *peeled and grated*

2 scallions *minced*

1 fresh hot chili pepper *minced* **(optional)**

1 lemon *cut into wedges*

shoyu

Miso-Marinated Grilled Porgy

Tai no Saikyo-yaki

Miso is often used to preserve fish, meat, and vegetables, as well as for flavoring. For fish, Saikyo (a white miso) is ideal as it is light and won't overwhelm the delicate flavor of the fish. White fish such as cod and flounder can also be used for this dish. **Serves 4**

4 porgy (or any white fish) fillets

For the marinade:

3½ ounces white *miso* (about 7 tablespoons)

3 tablespoons *sake*

2 tablespoons *mirin*

To serve:

selection of green vegetables

1 Mix together the white *miso*, *sake*, and *mirin* to make the marinade.

2 Spread half the marinade thinly over a flat plate and cover with a sheet of paper towel. Place the fish fillets, meat side down, on the paper and cover the fish with another sheet of paper towel. Spread the rest of the marinade over to cover the fish. (Using paper towel prevents the fish from becoming too salty, and it makes it easier to clean the *miso* from the fish.) Leave to marinate for 3–5 hours. (The longer the fish is marinated, the saltier it becomes.)

3 Remove the paper towel. Grill the fillets over a charcoal fire, or cook under the broiler, for 3–5 minutes or until cooked through and both sides are golden brown. (If grilling, thread each fillet on a metal skewer or use a fish grill.) Serve garnished with green vegetables.

Assorted Fishballs Hotpot

Oden

Except at festivals, nowadays oden *is the only street food still actually eaten on the street in Japan.* Oden *stalls appear at busy street corners after dark, to catch businessmen and workers on their way home after drinking in the bars. The dish is very easy to make at home because the main ingredients are ready-to-cook fish products obtainable in packets at Asian markets. The* oden *packet normally contains* chikuwa *(grilled fish stick with a hole),* gammodoki *(fried thick tofu),* hanpen *(fish cakes), fish balls,* gobo- *or* ika-maki *(fish rolls with burdock or squid),* konbu, *and condensed soup stock.* **Serves 4–6**

1 Cut the *konnyaku* across in half and then cut each piece into 4 triangles.

2 Wipe the *konbu* with damp paper towel, then soak in water for 10 minutes. Drain. Cut across in half and then into ½-inch ribbons. Tie each ribbon into a knot at the center.

3 Cut the *daikon* in half lengthwise and then across into 1 inch thick half-moons. If turnips are used, trim the stem part and quarter them; if large, cut the quarters in half. Cook the *daikon* or turnip pieces in boiling water until tender; drain. Parboil the potatoes; drain.

4 In a large earthenware or cast-iron pot, heat the chicken stock over low heat. Add the condensed soup stock from the packet of *oden*. Alternatively, if you make the soup yourself, add the *shoyu* and *mirin* (or *sake* and sugar) to the chicken stock and season with salt. Add all the prepared ingredients, including the eggs, if using, and the fish products, to the pot and simmer, uncovered, for 1 hour.

5 Bring the pot to the dining table and allow diners to help themselves onto individual plates. Eat with a little mustard.

1 x 8-ounce cake *konnyaku* (optional)

an 8- by 4-inch piece of *konbu* (optional)

½ large *daikon* or 4 turnips (1 pound) *peeled*

2–3 potatoes (10 ounces) *peeled and halved or quartered if large*

4 eggs *hard boiled and shelled* **(optional)**

1 packet of assorted fish products for *oden* (1⅔–2 pounds)

For the soup:

1 quart chicken stock

3 tablespoons *shoyu*

5 tablespoons *mirin*, or use 5 tablespoons *sake* plus 2 tablespoons sugar

1 teaspoon sea salt

To serve:

prepared English mustard

Tofu Steak with Daikon and Chili Sauce
Tofu no Steak

When cooking tofu this way, you need to squeeze out some of the liquid to make it firm. Then it can be handled without breaking. This makes a surprisingly filling dish, and is very attractive in its presentation. **Serves 4**

2 x 10-ounce cakes firm tofu

4 okra (about 2 ounces)

sea salt and freshly ground black pepper

all-purpose flour

vegetable oil for frying

1 medium eggplant *cut into ¹/₂ inch thick rounds*

shoyu

For the *momiji-oroshi*:

a 4-inch piece of large daikon (about 9 ounces) *peeled*

1–2 fresh hot red chili peppers *halved lengthwise and seeded*

1 Press the tofu (see page 29).

2 Meanwhile, cook the okra in lightly salted boiling water for 2–3 minutes; drain and rinse under cold running water. Cut off the hard stem part and then slice into thin rounds.

3 Make the *momiji-oroshi* (grated maple leaf) with the *daikon* and chili (see page 43).

4 Cut the cakes of pressed tofu in half horizontally, and sprinkle with salt and pepper. Dredge in flour and pat off any excess.

5 Heat a frying pan with 1 tablespoon of oil. Fry the tofu slices, one at a time, for 4–5 minutes or until golden brown on both sides, adding a little more oil each time. Add another tablespoon of oil to the pan and fry the eggplant slices for about 2 minutes or until both sides are golden brown.

6 Arrange one-fourth of the fried eggplant slices and a tofu steak on each of 4 individual plates. Put one-fourth of the *momiji-oroshi* on top of each steak. Sprinkle a little *shoyu* over the *momiji-oroshi*, and add one-fourth of the okra to each plate. Serve hot.

Ginger Pork

Butaniku no Shoga-yaki

This simple yet mouthwatering dish is particularly popular among youngsters. It's very quick to make (less than 30 minutes), quite filling, and cheap. It can be found on the menu at any Japanese street café. **Serves 4**

1⅔ **pounds boned pork loin chops**

a 2-inch piece of fresh ginger
peeled and grated

4 **tablespoons** *shoyu*

2–3 **tablespoons vegetable oil**

To serve:

salad leaves

1 Trim the pork chops and cut crosswise into very thin slices about 2 by 1 inch, inserting the blade almost horizontally. Spread the slices on a large plate. Sprinkle evenly with the grated ginger, along with its juice, and the *shoyu*. Leave to marinate for 10 minutes.

2 Heat a frying pan and add the oil. Pan-fry the marinated pork slices for 3 minutes on each side, or until thoroughly cooked and golden brown.

3 Arrange the cooked pork slices on a bed of salad leaves on each of 4 individual plates and serve.

Pork Steak Steam-Roasted with Ginger Miso

Buta no Shoga-miso Mushi-yaki

In Japanese cooking, miso *is used in innumerable ways, such as in soups, sauces, and marinades. Mixing ginger and* sake *with* miso *reduces the saltiness. This is another very easy dish to cook at home, and goes well with boiled rice.* **Serves 4**

1 Slice each pork steak horizontally in half, cutting from the lean side through to the fat edge, but not cutting all the way through. Sprinkle both sides of the pork with salt and pepper.

2 Mix together the *miso*, *sake*, and grated ginger (with its juice) in a small cup. Spread 1–2 teaspoonfuls of the ginger *miso* evenly over one cut surface of each pork slice, then press back together to make 4 pork steak and ginger *miso* sandwiches.

3 Place the pork steaks in a lightly oiled baking dish and cover with a sheet of foil. Cook in a preheated oven at 400°F for 20 minutes or until thoroughly cooked. Alternatively, wrap the steaks in a foil packet and grill over a moderate charcoal fire for about 20 minutes.

4 Slice each steak crosswise into 4–5 strips and arrange a steak on a bed of spinach on each of 4 individual plates. Spoon some of the cooking juices over and serve immediately.

4 pork steaks or boned loin chops (1⅔ pounds)

sea salt and freshly ground black pepper

1½ tablespoons *miso*

1 tablespoon *sake*

a 1-inch piece of fresh ginger *peeled and grated*

To serve:

spinach *lightly cooked*

Fried Pork Cutlet

Tonkatsu

One of the most popular single-dish restaurants in Japan is "Tonkatsu-ya" ("ya" is a shop or restaurant) where you choose between "ordinary" (boneless pork chop), "fillet," or "loin" cutlets. The fried pork is almost always served very simply garnished with shredded raw cabbage and a lemon wedge. **Serves 4**

1 Make a few slits into the fat of the pork cutlets (or chops) to prevent them from curling during cooking. Sprinkle with salt and pepper, then dredge in flour and shake off any excess. Dip in the beaten eggs and coat with bread crumbs.

2 Heat oil for deep-frying to 350°F. Gently slide the pork cutlets into the hot oil, 1 or 2 at a time, and deep-fry for 7–10 minutes, turning once or twice, until well cooked and golden brown all over. Remove and drain on a wire rack or paper towels.

3 While the pork is being fried, mix together the tomato ketchup and Worcestershire sauce in a small serving bowl.

4 Place the fried cutlets on a cutting board and cut each one across into pieces 1 inch wide. Make a bed of very finely shredded raw cabbage on individual plates, put a sliced pork cutlet on top, and garnish with lemon wedges. Serve with the *tonkatsu* sauce and a pot of mustard for extra pungency.

4 boned pork loin chops (about 1½ pounds)

sea salt and freshly ground black pepper

all-purpose flour

2 eggs *beaten*

dry bread crumbs

vegetable oil for deep-frying

For the *tonkatsu* sauce:

5 tablespoons tomato ketchup

1 tablespoon Worcestershire sauce

To serve:

finely shredded white cabbage

lemon wedges

prepared English mustard

Beef Tataki

Gyuniku no Tataki

This dish treats beef as if it's sashimi. *The beef is broiled and then marinated in a citrus sauce for 3 hours, making a very refreshing dish that is particularly good for hot summer days.* **Serves 4**

1 pound lean boneless sirloin steak

sea salt and freshly ground black pepper

For the marinade:

½ onion *thinly sliced into half-moons*

½ lemon *peeled and cut into rounds*

1 garlic clove *thinly sliced*

⅔ cup rice vinegar or white wine vinegar

7 tablespoons *shoyu*

4 tablespoons *sake*

To serve:

salad leaves

a 2½-inch piece of large *daikon* **(5 ounces)** *grated*

shoyu

1 Rub a pinch each of salt and pepper into the steak. Broil, close to the heat, until browned on both sides. Do not overcook—the beef should be rare inside. You can test by pressing the steak with your finger; it should be springy. Immediately plunge into ice water and rub off any burnt parts in the water. Drain and pat dry with paper towels.

2 Mix together the marinade ingredients in a mixing bowl. Add the steak and leave to marinate for at least 3 hours.

3 Drain the steak and thinly slice. Arrange on a bed of salad leaves on 4 individual plates, and garnish each plate with the grated *daikon* mixed with some *shoyu*.

Steak with Sesame-Miso Paste

Gyuniku no Goma-miso Yaki

The combination of miso *and sesame makes an excellent slightly sweet relish for meat and vegetables. Here, lightly broiled steak is enhanced by the unique flavor of* goma-miso, *served with okra and shiitake mushrooms. Simple and delicious canapés can be made by dipping salad vegetables such as cucumber, celery, and lettuce in* goma-miso. *This dish is also suitable for grilling.* **Serves 4**

1 With the tip of a knife, lightly score the steaks to prevent them from shrinking when cooked.

2 To make the *goma-miso* paste, crush the sesame seeds with a pestle in a small mixing bowl. Add the *miso*, sugar, *sake*, *mirin*, and *shoyu*. Blend well to a smooth paste, and set aside.

3 Place the okra and mushrooms on a rack in the broiler pan, and broil, about 5 inches from the heat, for about 2 minutes, or until lightly seared all over. Remove from the rack and keep warm.

4 Place the steaks on the rack and thinly smear the *goma-miso* paste over them. Broil until cooked to your liking, then turn the steaks over. Smear the *goma-miso* paste on the other side and continue broiling. Don't put the steaks too close to the heat, because *miso* is easily burnt. If grilling, first lightly grill the steaks on one side, then turn them over and baste the cooked side with the *goma-miso*. Grill the second side, then turn and baste again. Turn once more to dry the paste.

5 Remove from the heat and cut the steaks crosswise into strips about 1 inch thick. Serve on individual plates garnished with the okra and mushrooms.

4 filet mignon or boneless sirloin steaks (1⅔ pounds)

12 okra *stems trimmed*

8 fresh shiitake mushrooms or button mushrooms *stems trimmed*

For the *goma-miso* paste:

2 tablespoons sesame seeds

1¼ tablespoons *miso*

⅔ tablespoon sugar

1 tablespoon *sake*

1 tablespoon *mirin*

1 teaspoon *shoyu*

Beef Griddle with Onion Rings
Oil-yaki

Cooking at the table is an important feature of Japanese cuisine, and both restaurants and homes are well equipped for this. In the West, electric griddles or hot plates can be used for this dish. You can also cook it in the kitchen and then bring to the table. **Serves 4**

1 pound boneless beef sirloin or round *in one piece*

2 Spanish onions *cut into thin rings*

½ cup watercress sprigs

1 lemon *quartered*

vegetable oil

a 4-inch piece of large *daikon* (about 9 ounces) *peeled and grated*

shoyu

1 Trim any fat from the beef, then cut the piece lengthwise in half. Freeze the two pieces separately in freezer bags for at least 2 hours or overnight.

2 Partially thaw the frozen beef for about 30 minutes, or until the outside just begins to soften. Then cut each piece of beef across into slices, as thinly as you can. Arrange the beef slices decoratively on a platter.

3 On a second platter, arrange the onion rings with the watercress and lemon quarters.

4 Place a lightly oiled hot plate in the center of the dining table set with small individual plates. Serve the meat and vegetable platters accompanied by the grated *daikon* and *shoyu* in separate dishes. Diners mix their own dipping sauce, made from the grated *daikon*, lemon juice, and *shoyu*, and cook their own portion of meat and vegetables. Alternatively, pan-fry the beef and onions in the kitchen, and divide among 4 individual plates. Garnish each with a lemon wedge and watercress, and serve immediately, with the *daikon* and a pitcher of *shoyu*.

Chicken Teriyaki

Tori no Teriyaki

"Teriyaki" means to grill or braise with a glowing effect. The sugar content in the sauce gives the glow, so its inevitable slightly sweet taste makes the dish very popular with children as well as adults. The chicken can also be grilled over charcoal. **Serves 4**

1 pound chicken thighs
boned

cornstarch

vegetable oil for pan-frying

2 tablespoons sugar

2 tablespoons *mirin*

2 tablespoons *sake*

2½ tablespoons *shoyu*

4 scallions *cut into 2-inch pieces*

sea salt

1 Place the chicken thighs on a cutting board skin side up and, with a fork, prick the skin a few times (this will prevent it from shrinking during cooking). Lightly rub cornstarch all over the chicken.

2 Heat 2 tablespoons of oil in a frying pan over high heat. Put the chicken thighs in the pan, skin side down, and pan-fry until golden brown. Turn them over, lower the heat, and cook, covered, until thoroughly cooked.

3 Skim any excess oil from the pan, then add the sugar, *mirin*, *sake*, and *shoyu*. Spoon the juice over the chicken and gently shake the pan so that the juice spreads evenly.

4 In another pan, fry the scallions in a little oil until tender. Sprinkle with a little salt. Keep hot.

5 Place the chicken thighs on a cutting board and cut crosswise into ½-inch slices. Arrange on 4 individual plates, spoon the cooking juice over, and garnish with the scallions.

Steamed Chicken

Tori no Rikyu-ni

Japanese cuisine is renowned for its healthy fat-free style of cooking. When food is fried, the oiliness is often counteracted by dipping or marinating in a sauce. Here, the fat of chicken is doubly reduced by frying, marinating, and then steaming. No chicken can be healthier than this one. **Serves 4**

1 Heat a nonstick frying pan, or an ordinary pan with a little oil, and pan-fry the chicken breasts on high heat, skin side first, for 3–4 minutes on each side, or until light golden brown. Drain on paper towels.

2 In a shallow dish, mix together the *shoyu*, *mirin*, and *sake*. Lay the chicken breasts in the dish, skin side up. Leave to marinate for 20 minutes, then turn over and marinate for a further 10 minutes.

3 Transfer the marinated chicken breasts, skin side up, to a shallow flat-based dish and put on a rack in a steamer. Steam on high heat for about 10 minutes, then turn the chicken over and continue to steam for 7 minutes. Alternatively, put the chicken in a casserole and place it in a larger, deeper roasting pan, one-third filled with boiling water. Cover the whole with a large sheet of foil, and cook in a preheated oven at 400°F for 25 minutes, or until well cooked.

4 Drain, keeping the juice from the chicken warm, and put the breasts back in the marinade for 2–3 minutes. Transfer the chicken breasts to a cutting board and, with a sharp knife, cut crosswise into ¼ inch thick slices.

5 Arrange one sliced breast on each individual plate, spoon some of the cooking juice over, and serve with cooked broccoli.

4 boneless chicken breasts (1¼ pounds) *trimmed*

vegetable oil for pan-frying

6 tablespoons *shoyu*

7 tablespoons *mirin*

4 tablespoons *sake*

To serve:

broccoli *cooked*

Hand-Rolled Sushi

Temaki-zushi

All the components of this dish are prepared and served on the table, and the rest is done by the diners—a very convenient way of serving food for a host and fun for the guests. You can use any ingredients you like, even sausages and cheeses. Avocado is a good alternative to fish for vegetarians. **Serves 4**

1 Make the *sumeshi* (see page 13). Leave to cool.

2 Cut the smoked salmon into roughly 2- by 1-inch squares. Halve the *takuan*, or cucumber, crosswise and cut each piece into 8 sticks. Sprinkle a little *sake* and *shoyu* over the caviar. Arrange the smoked salmon, *takuan*, or cucumber, caviar, and crab sticks decoratively on a platter and garnish with pickled ginger.

3 Cut 6 of the *nori* sheets into quarters. Cut each of the remaining 2 sheets into 6 strips 1 inch wide. Place 6 squares and 3 strips on each of 4 individual plates.

4 Take about 1 heaped tablespoonful of the *sumeshi* in your hands and lightly squeeze into an oval shape. Repeat this until all the *sumeshi* is used. Arrange the *sumeshi* on a platter.

5 Serve the platters of seafood and *sumeshi* on the dining table set with small individual plates, together with the plates of *nori*, the *wasabi* paste on a separate plate, and a pitcher of *shoyu*. Diners spread a portion of *sumeshi* over a square of *nori*, with a little *wasabi*, wrap this around their choice of seafood, and eat, dipping in *shoyu*. For the strips of *nori*, place a ball of *sumeshi* on a plate, wrap a *nori* strip around it in the shape of a chef's hat, and put the caviar in the "hat."

4 ounces smoked salmon

a 4-inch piece of *takuan* (pickled daikon) or English cucumber

3 ounces lumpfish roe or salmon caviar

sake

shoyu

8 crab sticks (about 4½ ounces) *cut in half lengthwise*

Pickled Ginger (see page 104)

8 sheets of dried *nori*

***wasabi* paste**

For the *sumeshi* (vinegared rice):

2¼ cups Japanese rice

6 tablespoons rice vinegar or white wine vinegar

1 tablespoon sugar

1¼ teaspoons sea salt

Mixed Sushi Rice

Chirashi-zushi

Sumeshi (vinegared rice) mixed with various cooked ingredients makes a delicious lunch as well as an attractive party dish. This version is very simple to make. **Serves 4–6**

1 small carrot (about 3 inches long)

3–4 dried shiitake mushrooms

2½ tablespoons sugar

1½ tablespoons *shoyu*

½ x 7-ounce can tuna in brine or water *drained*

2 eggs

pinch of sea salt

vegetable oil

6 tablespoons green peas *cooked*

For the *sumeshi* (vinegared rice):

2¼ cups Japanese rice

6 tablespoons rice vinegar or white wine vinegar

1 tablespoon sugar

1¼ teaspoons sea salt

1 Make the *sumeshi* (see page 13). Leave to cool.

2 Cut the carrot in half crosswise. Thinly slice each piece lengthwise and then cut into shreds. Soak the shiitake in warm water for 30 minutes. Drain, reserving the liquid, and cut each shiitake into fine shreds.

3 Mix 1½ tablespoons of the sugar and the *shoyu* with 7 tablespoons of the shiitake soaking liquid and bring to a boil. Add the shiitake shreds and cook gently for 10 minutes. Add the carrot shreds and cook for a further 5 minutes. Remove from the heat and leave to cool in the liquid.

4 Put the tuna into a saucepan and add the remaining sugar. Cook on medium heat, flaking with the back of a fork, for 15–20 minutes or until the tuna becomes dry, fine, flaky granules. Set aside.

5 Beat 1 egg with the salt. Heat a lightly oiled 7-inch frying pan and pour in the egg, tilting the pan so that the egg spreads evenly over the bottom to make a paper-thin omelet. Fry over the lowest possible heat for 30 seconds or until the surface of the omelet is dry. Turn the omelet onto a board. Repeat with the other egg to make a second omelet. Cut into thin strips 2 inches long.

6 With a wooden spatula, fold the carrot and shiitake shreds, and half of the tuna granules, omelet strips, and peas into the *sumeshi*. Do not mash the rice. Pile in a serving dish and garnish with the remaining tuna granules, omelet strips, and peas on top.

Fried Tofu Bag Sushi

Inari-zushi

Abura-age is a very thin, fried tofu. It is slightly rubbery, which gives an interesting contrast of texture when it is cooked with vegetables. Here abura-age *is used in an unusual way— as a bag in which to stuff* sumeshi, *making quite a filling picnic or party dish.* **Serves 4**

1 Make the *sumeshi* (see page 13). Leave to cool.

2 If fresh *abura-age* is used, cut each in half crosswise and open up each half piece from the cut edge to make 16 bags. Reverse 8 of them inside out. Put all the pieces in boiling water and cook on medium heat for 4–5 minutes to reduce the oiliness. Drain.

3 Mix the sugar, *mirin*, *shoyu*, salt, and *dashi* granules with ⅔ cup water in a saucepan. Add the fresh *abura-age* halves. Cook on medium heat for 10 minutes, or until most of the liquid is absorbed. Remove from the heat and, when cool, drain. If canned *abura-age* is used, just drain them, open up the halves, and reverse 8 of them inside out.

4 Put the sesame seeds in a small saucepan and toss over medium heat until they start popping up. Remove from the heat and roughly crush in a mortar with a pestle. Mince half of the pickled ginger.

5 Using a wooden spatula, fold the sesame seeds and minced ginger into the *sumeshi*. Divide the mixture into 16 balls. Stuff a ball of rice into each bag of *abura-age*, and serve on a platter garnished with the remaining pickled ginger.

8 fresh *abura-age* or
1 x 9½-ounce can ready-to-use *abura-age* (16 halves)

½ cup sugar

2 tablespoons *mirin*

3 tablespoons *shoyu*

⅓ teaspoon sea salt

⅓ teaspoon *dashi* granules

2 tablespoons sesame seeds

3 ounces Pickled Ginger (see page 104)

For the *sumeshi* (vinegared rice):

1 cup + 2 tablespoons Japanese rice

2½ tablespoons rice vinegar or white wine vinegar

½ tablespoon sugar

⅔ teaspoon sea salt

Lunch Box

Bento

Bento, or, more politely, o'bento, is a unique feature of Japan's street food culture. It started at home, as lunch for children and husbands to take to school or the workplace, but quickly developed far beyond this, and you can now buy a vast range of bento *everywhere—including theaters and restaurants. Even provincial railway stations sell their own specialty* bento *using local produce. Here is an example of the basic homemade* bento. *You can pack the rice and other dishes in one large lunch box, but it's nicer to have separate boxes.* **Serves 2**

1½ cups Japanese rice

1 teaspoon black sesame seeds

2 eggs *beaten*

2 tablespoons chicken stock

2 teaspoons sugar

2 tablespoons chopped scallion

1 teaspoon minced fresh ginger

salt and pepper

vegetable oil for frying

1 portion of Chicken Teriyaki (see page 66) *sliced*

4 ounces broccoli *cooked*

orange wedges

1 Cook the rice (see page 13). Divide between 2 lunch boxes or plastic food containers. Sprinkle the black sesame seeds over the rice and leave uncovered until cold.

2 Mix together the eggs, chicken stock, sugar, scallion, and ginger. Season with salt and pepper. Heat a 6- to 7-inch frying pan, add a little oil, and, with paper towel, spread the oil lightly over the bottom. Add one-third of the egg mixture and tilt the pan to spread it evenly. When the omelet is half cooked, tightly roll it up. Rub the empty part of the pan with the oiled paper towel, then pour in half of the remaining egg mixture. When this second omelet is half cooked, roll it up around the first rolled omelet. Repeat with the remaining egg mixture, then turn the egg roll onto a *makisu*. Roll the *makisu* around the egg roll to tighten it. Leave to cool in the *makisu*. When cold, cut the egg roll across into 4.

3 In 2 more lunch boxes, arrange half of the chicken *teriyaki* and broccoli plus 2 slices of egg roll in each box, to fill by about two-thirds. Place the orange wedges (for dessert) to fill each box, using a sheet of foil as a partition. (If you want to use just 1 lunch box per person, divide the separate ingredients with a piece of foil or a green salad leaf.)

Rice Balls

Onigiri

Onigiri, *hand-molded rice with an ingredient in the center, is the Japanese equivalent of the sandwich. Traditional filling ingredients are* umeboshi *(salted dry plum), grilled salted salmon, and* kezuribushi *(dried bonito flakes), but any salty food can be used to balance the plain rice. Here's a new version.* **Makes 12**

1 Cook the rice (see page 13).

2 Meanwhile, soak the *hijiki* in water for 10 minutes, or until fully expanded, then drain and put in a saucepan with the *mirin* and 1 tablespoon of *shoyu*. Cook on medium heat for 5 minutes. Set aside.

3 Mix together the anchovies and pickled onion. Add the *sake* and remaining *shoyu* to the salmon or tuna and toss to mix.

4 Put 2 tablespoonfuls of rice into a small cup. Make a well in the center of the rice and put in 1 teaspoon of the anchovy mixture. Add another 1 tablespoonful of rice and press to cover. Wet your hands and lightly rub with salt. Turn out the rice onto one hand and squeeze, shaping it into a flattened ball. Wrap a *nori* ribbon around the rice ball, if using. Make 3 more rice balls filled with anchovy, then another 4 filled with salmon or tuna but shaping into triangles.

5 Mix the *hijiki* with the remaining rice and divide into 4. Take a portion on your hand and squeeze, shaping it into a ball. Serve the rice balls and triangles on a platter garnished with some pickled vegetables. For a picnic, pack one of each kind in each lunch box.

2 cups Japanese rice

⅓ ounce dried *hijiki*

1 tablespoon *mirin*

2 tablespoons *shoyu*

½ x 2-ounce can anchovy fillets *drained and minced*

1 pickled onion *minced*

1 tablespoon *sake*

⅓ cup canned salmon or tuna *drained and flaked*

sea salt

1 sheet of dried *nori* *cut into 8 ribbons* **(optional)**

To serve:

Japanese pickled vegetables

Salmon and Egg Rice Bowl

Sake Donburi

With canned fish, this simple dish can be made in no time. It is an excellent lunch or snack for all ages. If you use cooked chicken instead of salmon, it is called oyako—*parent and child—Rice Bowl. White fish such as cod and monkfish can also be used.* **Serves 4**

2¼ cups Japanese rice

1½ x 7-ounce cans salmon or tuna chunks

2 medium onions *halved and cut into thin half-moons*

¼ teaspoon *dashi* granules

1 tablespoon *sake* or white wine

1 tablespoon *shoyu*

1½ tablespoons sugar

2–3 eggs *beaten*

To serve:

watercress

1 Cook the rice (see page 13). Keep hot.

2 Drain the canned salmon and roughly break up with a fork.

3 Heat 7 fluid ounces water in a large frying pan and add the onion slices and the *dashi* granules. Cook on medium heat for 2–3 minutes. Add the salmon, then season with the *sake*, *shoyu*, and sugar. Cook for a further 2–3 minutes, or until the onion slices are soft.

4 Divide the cooked rice among 4 individual bowls and pour 1 tablespoon of the juices from the pan over each portion. Keep hot.

5 Pour the beaten eggs over the salmon and onion mixture, tilting the pan so that the egg covers all the surface. Place a lid on the pan and cook for another 2 minutes.

6 Remove from the heat and place one-fourth of the cooked salmon and egg mixture on top of each portion of rice. Spoon the remaining cooking juices over and serve immediately, garnished with watercress.

Chicken and Bamboo Shoots Rice

Takikomi Gohan

There is nothing more cherished by the Japanese than a bowl of freshly boiled rice. There are numerous dishes of rice boiled with seasonal vegetables or shellfish, which not only add extra flavor to the rice, but also make it express the season in a subtle way. Here bamboo shoots and chicken are cooked with the rice. Boiled fresh bamboo shoots are best for this dish, although canned bamboo shoots can be used. **Serves 4**

1 Wash the rice thoroughly, changing the water 4 or 5 times until it becomes clear. Drain in a strainer and leave for 1 hour. (If you do not have time to do this, just soak the rice in water for 10 minutes and drain.)

2 Put the bamboo shoots in a large saucepan and add 1¼ cups of water, the *dashi* granules, *shoyu*, and *mirin*. Cook on medium heat for about 5 minutes. Drain the bamboo shoots, reserving the cooking liquid, and cut into chunky bite-sized pieces.

3 Place the washed and drained rice in a large earthenware or cast-iron saucepan and add the reserved bamboo shoot cooking liquid. Put the bamboo shoots and chicken pieces on top. Cover and cook on medium heat for 7–8 minutes, then lower the heat and cook for a further 20 minutes, or until the rice is tender and all the liquid has been absorbed.

4 Remove from the heat and leave to settle, still covered, for 15 minutes. Serve hot on individual plates.

1½ cups Japanese rice

10 ounces boiled fresh or canned bamboo shoot chunks *drained*

1 teaspoon *dashi* granules

2 tablespoons *shoyu*

2 tablespoons *mirin*

9 ounces skinless, boneless chicken thighs *trimmed and cut into 1-inch cubes*

main dishes

Rice Cakes with Chicken Soup
O'zoni

On New Year's Day, the Japanese always have o'zoni for brunch. There are several regional variations of this chicken soup with mochi *(rice cakes)—in the Tokyo area, in the east, they make a clear soup with square* mochi, *chicken, and a green vegetable, whereas in the Osaka area, in the west, they eat a more elaborate* miso *soup with round* mochi *and various vegetables. The recipe here is the simpler Tokyo version.* **Serves 4**

1 skinless, boneless chicken breast (about 4 ounces)
thinly sliced crosswise

sea salt

1 tablespoon *sake*

7 ounces fresh spinach leaves (about 2 cups)

1 teaspoon *dashi* granules

1 tablespoon *shoyu*

4 *mochi* *cut across in half*

To serve:

finely shredded lime zest

1 Sprinkle the slices of chicken with a pinch of salt and the *sake*. Set aside.

2 Cook the spinach in boiling water for 30 seconds, then drain and immediately put under cold running water to stop further cooking. Squeeze out excess water and cut roughly into bite-sized pieces.

3 Bring 2½ cups of water to a boil in a saucepan. Add the *dashi* granules and season with 1 teaspoon of salt and the *shoyu*. Add the chicken slices and cook for 2 minutes or until the chicken turns white.

4 Toast the *mochi* under the broiler, about 5 inches from the heat, for 4–5 minutes or until light golden brown on both sides.

5 Place 2 pieces of *mochi* in each of 4 individual soup bowls and put one-fourth of the spinach and chicken slices on top. Pour the soup over and serve immediately, garnished with shredded lime zest.

78

Toasted Rice Cake with Cheese

Yaki Mochi

Mochi, or more politely o'mochi, are the most important item for New Year's feasts. They are made by pounding steamed glutinous rice in a wooden mortar and then forming into cakes, balls, and other shapes, in varying sizes. In the past, mochi *pounders, pulling a cart with a huge wooden mortar and pestle, called house to house every December. Nowadays, various types of ready-made* mochi *are easily obtainable all year round, the most common being oblong pieces, about 1¼ by 2 inches and ½ inch thick, individually vacuum-wrapped. Here's a simple but delicious snack dish.* **Serves 4**

8 mochi (14 ounces)
cut across in half

shoyu

4 ounces Cheddar or any other hard cheese

2 sheets of dried *nori* (optional)

1 Toast the *mochi* under the broiler, about 5 inches from the heat, turning them over frequently, for 2–3 minutes, or until both sides are light golden brown. Coat both sides with *shoyu* and put back under the broiler, a bit farther from the heat. Toast for 10 seconds on each side. Coat with *shoyu* and toast each side again for 2–3 seconds, or until dry.

2 Cut the cheese into 8 pieces of a similar size to the *mochi*. Make a slit horizontally in the center of each toasted *mochi* and stuff with a piece of cheese.

3 Cut each *nori* sheet into quarters. Wrap each cheese-stuffed *mochi* with a piece of *nori*. Serve all on a platter.

Udon with Curry Soup

Curry Udon

Curry houses are found everywhere in Japan. In fact, curry is so popular that the Japanese have invented a curry "roux"—a condensed curry sauce that is available in Japanese supermarkets—to speed up the process of making curry. You only need to cook fresh ingredients in water; the thickening and flavoring are all done by the roux. Here is a dish of udon *served in curry soup.* **Serves 4**

1 Cook the *udon* following package directions. Immediately rinse under cold running water to wash away the outer starch. Drain.

2 If making the soup with curry roux, bring 2½ cups of water to a boil in a saucepan, add the curry roux, and stir until dissolved. Add the *shoyu*. Without the curry roux, mix the curry powder with a little of the chicken stock, then add to the remaining stock, along with the sugar and *shoyu*. Bring to a boil.

3 Cook the chicken in the boiling soup for 3–4 minutes, then add the scallions and cook for a further 30 seconds. Remove the chicken and scallions with a slotted spoon and divide into 4 portions; keep hot. Check the seasoning of the soup and add salt, if necessary. If the soup was made without the roux, add the cornstarch mixture and cook to thicken, stirring.

4 Pour boiling water over the cooked *udon* to refresh, then divide among 4 individual *udon* bowls. Place a portion of chicken and scallions on top of each *udon* bowl and ladle some soup over. Serve hot, garnished with cress on top.

1 pound dried *udon*

2 skinless, boneless chicken breasts or 3 skinless, boneless thighs (9 ounces) *cut into small pieces*

2 scallions *cut in half lengthwise then into 2-inch pieces*

sea salt

For the soup (with curry roux):

3½ ounces curry roux

1 tablespoon *shoyu*

For the soup (without curry roux):

2 teaspoons curry powder

2½ cups chicken stock

1 tablespoon sugar

1 tablespoon *shoyu*

1 tablespoon cornstarch *mixed with 2 tablespoons water*

To serve:

cress

Cold Soba

Zaru Soba

The Japanese cannot survive, even for a few days, without a bowl of noodles, whether soba *(made from buckwheat flour),* somen *and* udon *(both wheat flour), or* ramen *(Chinese-style egg noodles). So it's not surprising to come across a Soba-ya (noodle shop) every 10 yards or so on any high street in Japan.* Soba *are regarded as health food and are becoming increasingly popular in the West. Here is a quite basic* soba *dish.* **Serves 4**

1 Cook the *soba* in plenty of boiling water, following the directions on the package. Drain and rinse away the starch from the noodles, changing the water 2 or 3 times. Drain well and set aside.

2 Very lightly toast the *nori* on both sides by holding the sheet about 2 inches over a very low heat for 2–3 seconds (toasting brings out the flavor as well as crisping up the *nori*). Crush into pieces on paper towel, or use scissors to cut into thin shreds about 1 inch long.

3 To make the dipping sauce, heat 1¼ cups of water in a saucepan and add the *shoyu*, *mirin*, and sugar. Simmer over medium heat until the sugar dissolves, then lower the heat and add the *dashi* granules. Stir until dissolved. Half fill 4 small individual bowls or cups with the sauce. (Serve the dip chilled in summer.)

4 If powdered *wasabi* is used, mix it with the same amount of water to make a firm paste. Put the *wasabi* onto a small plate or dish.

5 Rinse the *soba* under cold running water; drain and arrange on 4 individual bamboo mats placed on large plates, or directly onto individual plates. Sprinkle the *soba* with the *nori*. Serve with the dipping sauce, *wasabi*, and scallions. Diners mix *wasabi* and scallions into their own sauce and then dip in the *soba*.

1 pound dried *soba*

½ **sheet of dried** *nori*

4 teaspoons *wasabi* **paste or powder**

2 scallions *minced*

For the dipping sauce:

5 tablespoons *shoyu*

3 tablespoons *mirin*

1 tablespoon sugar

½ teaspoon *dashi* **granules**

Mushroom Ramen

Kinoko Ramen

A ramen dish is ideal when you want a quick but nutritious lunch or snack. It's also extremely convenient, as any ingredients can be used. Here's a version with an appetizing salty taste, rather than the usual shoyu flavoring. **Serves 4**

6–8 fresh or dried shiitake mushrooms *stems trimmed*

2 ounces *enoki* or oyster mushrooms

2 ounces button mushrooms

2–3 tablespoons vegetable oil

sea salt and freshly ground black pepper

1 ounce dried *wakame* or 4 ounces spinach (about 1 cup) *trimmed*

9 ounces dried *ramen*

For the broth:

5 cups chicken or vegetable stock

a 1-inch square piece of fresh ginger *crushed*

1½ teaspoons salt

2 teaspoons *shoyu*

pepper

To serve:

1 scallion *minced*

1 If dried shiitake are used, soak in warm water for 30 minutes; drain.

2 Cut the shiitake and large oyster mushrooms in half and the button mushrooms into 4–5 slices. If using *enoki* mushrooms, trim off the hard stem part and separate into individual pieces. Heat the oil in a frying pan and stir-fry all the mushrooms together on high heat for 2 minutes. Lightly season with salt and pepper, and remove from the heat.

3 Soak the *wakame* in water for 10 minutes until fully opened, then drain. Blanch in boiling water for 1 minute; drain and squeeze out excess water. If the *wakame* is not already cut, chop into ¾- to 1¼-inch lengths. If spinach is used, place in a large mixing bowl and pour boiling water over. Stir once or twice so that all the leaves wilt, then drain and squeeze out excess water.

4 Put the stock and ginger in a saucepan and bring to a boil. Season the stock with the salt, *shoyu*, and pepper. Simmer for 10 minutes, then discard the ginger.

5 Cook the *ramen* until just soft, following package directions. Immediately rinse away the outer starch under cold running water. Drain and divide among 4 individual noodle bowls. Arrange the mushrooms and *wakame* (or spinach) on top of the noodles and pour in the broth. Serve immediately, garnished with minced scallion.

Miso Ramen with Seafood

Gyokai-iri Miso Ramen

Miso ramen *was invented in Sapporo, capital city of Hokkaido, the most northern island, but is now eaten all over Japan. Hokkaido has a very cold climate, which explains the addition of* miso—*it not only gives the broth a strong taste, but also warms the body. It is further enhanced by the addition of grated garlic. Hokkaido is also well known for its seafood.* **Serves 4**

1 Skin the squid (see page 23). Cut the squid body in half lengthwise. Place one half on a cutting board, skin side down, and make shallow cuts in a criss-cross pattern on the surface. Repeat this process with the other half. Cut into 1- by 2-inch pieces. Cut the flaps in half. Separate the tentacles and cut into ¾ inch long pieces. Cook all the squid pieces in boiling water over medium heat for 1–2 minutes. Drain.

2 Cut the *hakusai* leaves in half lengthwise, then finely shred crosswise. Stir-fry with a little oil in a frying pan or wok on high heat for 3–4 minutes or until wilting but still crunchy. Season with salt and pepper. Set aside.

3 To make the broth, heat the chicken stock with the ginger and simmer for 10 minutes. Discard the ginger. Dilute the *miso* with some of the broth, then add to the pan. Season with the *shoyu*, and salt and pepper to taste.

4 Cook the *ramen* until just soft, following package directions. Immediately rinse away the outer starch under cold running water. Drain and divide among 4 individual noodle bowls. Arrange one-fourth of the squid, shrimp, baby clams, and *hakusai* on top of each bowl of noodles and pour in the broth. Serve immediately, garnished with watercress or cress, with grated garlic in a separate small bowl.

1 small squid (12 ounces) *cleaned*

2–3 *hakusai* leaves (Napa cabbage)

vegetable oil for frying

sea salt and freshly ground black pepper

9 ounces dried *ramen*

12–20 cooked peeled shrimp

1 x 6½-ounce can baby clams *drained*

For the broth:

5 cups chicken stock

a 1-inch piece of fresh ginger *crushed*

6 tablespoons *miso* (white, if available)

2 tablespoons *shoyu*

To serve:

watercress or cress

2 garlic cloves *grated*

Ramen with Pork

Shoyu Ramen

The Japanese have developed a wide range of dishes using Chinese-style egg noodles (ramen), *and even regional differences in cooking them. The* ramen *craze is so hot in Japan that there is a* ramen *museum, a* ramen *village, and even* ramen *appreciation clubs!* **Serves 4**

10 ounces boned loin of pork
in one piece

1 quart chicken stock

5 tablespoons *shoyu*

4 ounces fresh spinach leaves (about 1 cup)

1 cup bean sprouts

vegetable oil (optional)

sea salt and freshly ground black pepper

4 portions of dried *ramen* **(about 8 ounces)**

To serve:

1 scallion *minced*

1 Put the pork in a saucepan with the chicken stock and bring to a boil. Cook on medium heat for 10 minutes, constantly skimming the surface.

2 Remove the pork to another saucepan and add the *shoyu* and 5 tablespoons of the soup; keep the remaining soup hot. Cook the pork on medium heat for about 10 minutes. Remove from the heat and set aside.

3 Lightly boil the spinach, then drain and squeeze out the excess water with your hands. Chop the spinach into bite-sized pieces. Place the bean sprouts in a bowl and pour boiling water over. Leave for 5 minutes, then drain. Alternatively, stir-fry the bean sprouts in a little oil. Season with a pinch of salt and pepper.

4 Thinly slice the pork. Reserve the cooking juices.

5 Cook the *ramen* in boiling water according to the package directions, then rinse off the starch with cold water and drain.

6 Put 2 tablespoons of the juices from cooking the pork into each of 4 individual noodle bowls. Add the hot soup to half-fill the bowls. Put one-fourth each of the *ramen*, sliced pork, bean sprouts, and spinach on top. Sprinkle with pepper and serve garnished with scallion.

SIDE

DISHES

Fine Beans with Walnut Dressing

Ingen no Kurumimiso-ae

Sesame seeds, both black and white, are often used as a flavoring for sauces and dressings in Japanese cooking. Here I've replaced the more traditional sesame seeds with walnuts, to make a delicious dressing for beans. **Serves 4**

9 ounces haricots verts or other green beans *trimmed*

sea salt

For the dressing:

½ cup shelled walnuts

1 tablespoon sugar

1 tablespoon *shoyu*

1 tablespoon *sake* **or white wine**

1 Cut the beans diagonally into thin, 2 inch long strips. Cook in lightly salted boiling water for 1 minute. Drain and immediately put under cold running water to stop further cooking and to set the green color. Drain and roughly pat dry with paper towels.

2 To make the dressing, pound the walnuts in a mortar with a pestle into a dry, pastelike consistency. Transfer to a small bowl. Add the sugar, *shoyu*, and *sake*, and mix well. Add 2 tablespoons of water and stir until smooth. Check the seasoning, adding a pinch of salt, if required.

3 Put the beans in a mixing bowl, pour the walnut dressing over, and gently mix to coat the beans evenly. Arrange on a serving plate or in a salad bowl and serve.

Stir-Fried Parsnip with Chili

Parsnip Kinpira

Stir-fried shredded vegetables with chili is a very traditional Japanese dish, although the name Kinpira *suggests that its origin is probably Portuguese.* Gobo *(burdock), a stringy, gray-colored root vegetable, is normally used, but parsnip provides a good substitute.*
Serves 4

2 parsnips (10 ounces) *peeled*

1 small carrot *peeled*

vegetable oil

1–2 fresh hot red chili peppers *seeded and minced*

2 tablespoons *sake*

2 tablespoons *shoyu*

1 tablespoon sugar

sea salt

2 teaspoons toasted sesame oil

1 Cut the parsnips and carrot crosswise into pieces about 2 inches long. Thinly slice each piece lengthwise, then cut into strips.

2 Heat a large frying pan or wok and add a little oil, tilting the pan to spread it over the bottom. Stir in the chilies, then add the parsnip and carrot strips. Stir-fry over high heat for 3–4 minutes or until the vegetable strips begin to wilt.

3 Lower the heat and sprinkle the vegetables with the *sake*, *shoyu*, and sugar. Continue to stir-fry until the liquid is almost completely absorbed. Check the seasoning and add salt to taste. Add the sesame oil, toss, and serve immediately in a deep serving plate or salad bowl.

Potato Simmered with Meat

Nikujaga

Cooking meat may not be the strongest point in Japanese cooking, but cooking vegetables is. This simple dish combines the best of the two: the gentle cooking method for vegetables with the flavor of meat. Typical street food, this is quick and cheap. **Serves 4**

1 Parboil the potatoes in plenty of boiling water for 5–6 minutes or until almost soft but still firm. (Poke a toothpick or fork through a piece; the potato should feel a little hard inside.) Drain.

2 Stir-fry the pork or beef in a lightly oiled frying pan over high heat. When the meat no longer looks raw, add the potatoes and continue to stir-fry for 1 minute.

3 Sprinkle in the sugar, *shoyu*, and *mirin*. Add enough water to the pan so the meat and potatoes are just covered. Bring to a boil, then lower the heat and simmer, covered, on medium heat for 10 minutes.

4 Add the onions and simmer, still covered, for a further 3–4 minutes or until the onions are cooked.

5 Divide the meat, potatoes, and onions among 4 individual dishes, pour over a little of the cooking liquid, and serve immediately, garnished with 1–2 parsley sprigs.

5–6 medium potatoes (1 pound) *peeled and quartered*

9 ounces boneless pork or beef (any cut) *thinly sliced into bite-sized pieces*

vegetable oil

4 tablespoons sugar

5 tablespoons *shoyu*

2 tablespoons *mirin*

2 large onions *cut in half and then into ¼ inch wide strips*

To serve:

sprigs of parsley

Five Vegetables Cooked in Dashi

Gomoku-ni

This is the ultimate Japanese vegetable dish—five vegetables of different shapes, textures, and colors cooked in a dashi *sauce. Every street café and restaurant has its own version. The dish can be made in large quantities and kept for a few days.* **Serves 4**

1 Soak the shiitake in warm water to cover for 30 minutes. Drain, reserving the soaking liquid. Trim the stems, then cut the caps in half, or into quarters if large.

2 Cook the green beans in lightly salted boiling water for 1–2 minutes. Drain and place under cold running water. Drain again and cut in half.

3 Trim off any fat from the chicken and chop into bite-sized pieces. Heat a deep cast-iron pot over high heat and stir-fry the chicken in a little oil for 1 minute, or until it becomes white on the surface. Add 1 tablespoon each of *sake*, sugar, and *shoyu*; stir-fry for 2–3 minutes on medium heat until all the liquid is absorbed. Transfer to a plate.

4 Add more oil to the pot and stir-fry the shiitake, carrot, and turnips for 1 minute. Add 1 cup of the shiitake soaking liquid and ½ cup water. Bring to a boil. Add the *dashi* granules, then cover the pot and simmer the vegetables on medium heat for 5 minutes. Add the *satoimo* or potatoes and simmer for 7–8 minutes, or until the *satoimo* is just cooked.

5 Add the remaining *sake*, sugar, and *shoyu* to the pot along with the *mirin*. Return the chicken to the pot. Continue to simmer on low heat, uncovered, for 5–6 minutes or until all the liquid has been absorbed. About 30 seconds before removing from the heat, add the beans and stir to mix. Transfer to a large serving bowl and serve immediately.

4–5 dried shiitake mushrooms

2 ounces green beans *trimmed*

salt

3 chicken thighs (about 9 ounces) *skinned and boned*

vegetable oil

2 tablespoons *sake* or white wine

3 tablespoons sugar

3 tablespoons *shoyu*

1 medium carrot *cut into bite-sized pieces*

3 medium turnips *quartered*

½ teaspoon *dashi* granules

4–5 *satoimo* (eddoes or taro roots) or potatoes *peeled and cut in half if large*

1 tablespoon *mirin*

Salt-Steamed Kabocha Squash

Kabocha no Sio-mushi

Kabocha, the Japanese squash, has a very dense texture and when cooked it becomes fluffy, just like potatoes. In Japan, it's an indispensable part of the daily diet. Its delicately sweet taste can be best appreciated when the vegetable is cooked very simply. This is the basic, but best, cooking method. **Serves 4**

½ **kabocha squash
(about 1 pound 2 ounces)**
seeds and fibers removed

sea salt

1 Trim off the hard stem part of the squash and roughly scrape off some of the hard skin (about a fifth). The skin is delicious to eat, but cutting off some of it makes for a better balance of soft and hard textures. Cut the squash into 4 half-moons, then chop each into 2–3 chunky pieces.

2 Put 5 tablespoons water in a flat-based saucepan and lay the squash on the bottom. Sprinkle over a pinch of salt. Cover and cook on medium heat for 3–4 minutes. Then reduce the heat as low as possible and cook for a further 15 minutes. Remove from the heat and leave, still covered, to settle for 5 minutes.

3 Heap the squash in the center of a serving dish and provide a salt mill for additional seasoning to taste.

Sake-Simmered Sweet Potato

Satsumaimo no Saka-mushi

The type of sweet potato used in Japan is the "Satsuma" variety, which has a scarlet to dark red outer skin and light yellow flesh that is tender and sweet. Other sweet potatoes can be used for this dish, but a tender and sweet variety is best. **Serves 4**

2 medium sweet potatoes (1 pound) *cut into ¾-inch rounds*

½ cup demerara or other raw brown sugar

5 tablespoons *sake*

sea salt

shoyu

1 Soak the sweet potato slices in cold water, changing the water several times until clear. Drain.

2 Place the sweet potato slices in a frying pan or flat-based shallow saucepan and add enough water to come three-quarters of the way up the sides of the potato slices. Add the sugar, *sake*, and a pinch of salt. To prevent the liquid from evaporating too quickly, lay a small plate, or a sheet of parchment paper cut to fit, on top of the potatoes; put the lid on the pan. Bring to a boil over medium heat, then reduce the heat to low and simmer for about 15 minutes or until the sweet potatoes are tender.

3 Just before removing from the heat, remove the parchment paper from the pan and sprinkle the sweet potatoes with a little *shoyu* to add a touch of flavor. Leave to cool in the liquid until the sweet potatoes can be handled.

4 Carefully peel the skin off the potato slices, then arrange on a serving dish. Serve immediately, while still warm.

Grilled Eggplant with Ginger

Yaki Nasu

The Japanese eggplant, like all other Japanese vegetables (not to mention the people), is a lot smaller than Western varieties and it has a more delicate taste. Thus, in Japan, a whole eggplant would be grilled for this dish, rather than halved eggplant as here. **Serves 4**

1 Cut the eggplants lengthwise in half, keeping the stem intact on each piece. On each half, make a slit crosswise in the skin just below the stem and 5–6 fine vertical slits down from the stem, to enable the skin to be peeled off easily after cooking.

2 Grill the eggplant halves over a medium charcoal fire, flesh side first for 3–5 minutes, or until lightly golden brown, and then skin side for 7–10 minutes, or until almost charred. Immediately plunge into cold water, drain and peel off the skin. (Alternatively, cook under the broiler, about 5 inches from the heat.)

3 While the eggplant is being grilled, heat 7 tablespoons water in a saucepan and add the *dashi* granules, *shoyu*, and *mirin*. Bring to a boil, then immediately remove from the heat.

4 Arrange the eggplant halves on 4 individual dishes, pour some sauce over, and garnish with the ginger and mint. Serve immediately.

4 eggplants

½ teaspoon *dashi* granules

2½ tablespoons *shoyu*

2 tablespoons *mirin*

To serve:

a 2-inch piece of fresh ginger
peeled and grated

finely shredded fresh mint leaves

Daikon Cooked with Squid

Ika Daikon

Daikon simmered in dashi *sauce is one of the most popular dishes in Japan. When raw,* daikon *has a strong, peppery radish taste, but after cooking for a long time the flavor becomes more subtle and is very pleasant. Cooking with squid adds to its distinctive flavor.*

Serves 4

1 Cut the *daikon* crosswise into 1¼ inch thick rounds.

2 Skin the squid by holding the two flaps together with one hand and pulling them down and off the squid body. Discard the skin from the flaps. Cut the skinned squid body into ⅓ inch thick rings. Cut each flap in half. Separate the tentacles, cutting long ones in half. Put all the squid pieces in a mixing bowl and pour plenty of boiling water over to cover. Drain.

3 Put the *daikon* and squid in a deep saucepan and add 1¼ cups of water. Bring to a boil, then lower the heat and add the *dashi* granules. Simmer on low heat for 30 minutes, skimming the surface several times.

4 Add the sugar, *mirin*, and half the *shoyu*. Simmer for a further 10 minutes. Add the remaining *shoyu* and continue to simmer until the liquid has reduced by half.

5 Arrange one-fourth each of the *daikon* and squid, with the cooking liquid, in each of 4 individual bowls. Serve immediately, with mustard and *sansho* in separate dishes or jars for individual seasoning.

1 large *daikon* (about 1⅔ pounds) peeled

1 medium squid (about 1 pound) cleaned

1 teaspoon *dashi* granules

1 tablespoon sugar

4 tablespoons *mirin*

4 tablespoons *shoyu*

To serve:

prepared English mustard

powdered *sansho*

Pickled Ginger

Beni Shoga and Kine Shoga

Pickled ginger is used as an accompaniment for many Japanese dishes. Beni shoga *(red ginger, or* "gari" *in sushi-shop jargon), which is thinly sliced pickled ginger, is an essential accompaniment to* sushi. Kine shoga, *young spring ginger sticks pickled whole, often accompanies grilled dishes.* **Serves 6–12**

For *beni shoga*:

4 ounces fresh root ginger *peeled*

1 tablespoon sea salt

For *kine shoga*:

12 new ginger shoots with stems

For the marinade:

7 tablespoons rice vinegar or white wine vinegar

2–3 tablespoons sugar

1 For the marinade, mix the vinegar with 4 tablespoons water and sugar according to your taste, stirring until the sugar dissolves.

2 To make *beni shoga*, break the ginger into knobs and cut each knob lengthwise into paper-thin slices along the grain. Put the slices in a mixing bowl and rub in the salt. Leave for 2–3 hours until the ginger wilts. Drain and squeeze out all excess liquid by squashing between your hands (or in one fist if your hands are large). Pour the marinade over the ginger slices, covering them completely. Leave to marinate for at least 1–2 days; the ginger will turn pale pink. *Beni shoga* will keep fresh for up to 3 months, but it is best used within a month.

3 To make *kine shoga*, separate the ginger shoots and cut into about 4-inch lengths. Pour boiling water over the ginger, then drain. Put the marinade into a tall narrow glass or mug. Stand the ginger shoots in it and leave to marinate for 3–4 hours. Drain before using.

Radish Cherry Blossoms

Kabu no Sakura-zuke

In Japan, turnips are often pickled, but Western turnips are too tough to pickle, so I use radishes instead. The result is a pleasant surprise: a beautiful bunch of cherry blossoms— a perfect garnish for sushi *or other dishes.* **Makes 8 ounces**

1 Cut the stem off each radish to make a flat base. Lay a pair of cheap *hashi* or pencils parallel to each other, and to you, on a cutting board and place a radish in between, flat base down. Using a sharp knife, make 4–6 vertical cuts in the radish, cutting just until the blade touches the *hashi* (or pencils) so that the radish remains in one piece. Turn the radish 90 degrees and make a few more cuts across the cuts already made. Repeat this with all the remaining radishes.

2 Put the radishes in a bowl, sprinkle with the salt, and lightly rub in. Place a small plate, smaller than the bowl, directly on top of the radishes. Put a weight (such as a can of food) on the plate to press the radishes lightly and leave for 30 minutes.

3 Mix the rice vinegar with the sugar, stirring until the sugar dissolves.

4 Drain the liquid that will have run from the radishes, then pour the vinegar mixture over them. Leave to marinate at least overnight. Drain well before using, with watercress or green leaves, to decorate a dish.

8 ounces red radishes

1 teaspoon sea salt

7 fluid ounces rice vinegar

¾ cup sugar

Spinach and Watercress in Dashi Sauce

Horenso to Kureson no Ohitashi

For ohitashi, *vegetables are parboiled and then marinated in* dashi *and* shoyu—*an ideal method for appreciating the subtle flavor of the vegetables. You can use any greens, but spinach is the traditional and still most popular one for* ohitashi *in Japan. Here, the traditional soft spinach* ohitashi *is complemented by crunchy watercress.* **Serves 4**

1 Blanch the spinach in lightly salted boiling water, then drain and place under running water to cool down quickly. Squeeze out the excess water with your hands.

2 Blanch and drain the watercress in the same way, then cut roughly into pieces 2 inches long.

3 Mix together the *ohitashi* sauce ingredients with 7 tablespoons water in a large, flat-based dish like a serving dish, stirring until the *dashi* granules are dissolved. Add the spinach and watercress (do not mix) and leave to marinate in the sauce for 5–6 minutes.

4 Remove the spinach, lightly squeezing out the excess sauce, and place on a cutting board. Roughly line up the spinach leaves, piling them on top of each other, alternating the leaves and stems in different directions, to form an 8-inch long log shape that is 1½ inches thick. Cut across into 8 cylinders, each 1½ inches long.

5 Lightly toss the sesame seeds in a small saucepan on a high heat until the first seed pops up. Remove from the heat. Dip the flat faces of the spinach cylinders in the sesame seeds. Arrange in the center of a serving plate surrounded by the lightly drained watercress. Sprinkle the remaining sesame seeds over the watercress and garnish with a few radish cherry blossoms, if desired.

10 ounces fresh spinach (about 3 cups)

sea salt

5 ounces watercress (about 2 cups)

2 tablespoons white sesame seeds

For the *ohitashi* sauce:

½ teaspoon *dashi* granules

2 tablespoons *shoyu*

2 tablespoons *mirin*

To serve:

Radish Cherry Blossoms (see page 105) (optional)

Salted Hakusai

Hakusai no Shiozuke

In Japanese cooking, there were once many methods for preserving fresh produce during the severe winter months. One very traditional method, called nuka-zuke, *uses rice bran mash as a pickling agent. It is less popular nowadays, due to its laborious preparation and strong smell. However, preserving by salting still survives, as it's easy and also adds flavor. Here's a very basic example.* **Serves up to 20**

1 head *hakusai* (Napa cabbage) (10 ounces) *leaves separated and washed*

10 *shiso* (beefsteak leaves) or 20 basil leaves *cleaned and minced*

1–2 tablespoons sea salt

2–3 fresh hot red or green chili peppers *seeded and minced* **(optional)**

To serve:

finely shredded fresh ginger or lime zest

shoyu

1 Cut the *hakusai* leaves in half lengthwise, then across into 1-inch pieces.

2 Put 2 handfuls of *hakusai* into a large freezer bag and sprinkle in some of the chopped *shiso* or basil, ½ teaspoonful of salt, and a little chili, if using. Add another 2 handfuls of the *hakusai* on top and sprinkle with more herbs, salt, and chili. Repeat this process until all the ingredients are in the bag, evenly spread throughout.

3 Tie the bag firmly to make it airtight, then leave in the refrigerator to wilt. Every few hours, roughly squeeze out the water that will form, and gently turn around the ingredients at the same time so that the seasonings are spread evenly.

4 The *hakusai* will be ready to eat after 3–4 hours, but is best after 2–3 days; the longer it's salted the stronger the final flavor. It will keep for up to 5 days in the refrigerator. Serve in a salad bowl, garnished with ginger or lime zest and accompanied by a pitcher of *shoyu*.

Spinach with Mustard Dressing

Horenso no Karashi-ae

A lightly cooked vegetable with a pungent mustard dressing makes a refreshing accompaniment for meat dishes. Here spinach is used, a vegetable needing only brief cooking, so the dish can be ready within 5 minutes. **Serves 4**

1 Put the spinach in a large mixing bowl. Pour about 1 quart of boiling water over and gently turn so that all the leaves wilt. Drain and immediately put under cold running water to stop the spinach cooking any further. Drain and squeeze out the excess water with your hands.

2 Lay the spinach leaves horizontally on a cutting board, piling them on top of each other, alternating the leaves and stems in different directions to form a log shape about 8 inches long and 2 inches in diameter. Cut the "log" crosswise into pieces about 1½ inches long. Arrange the pieces, cut side up, on a serving plate or in 4 individual salad bowls.

3 Mix together the mustard, *shoyu*, *sake*, and vinegar in a small bowl, stirring until amalgamated. Pour the dressing over the spinach and serve.

1 pound fresh spinach *trimmed*

For the dressing:

1 teaspoon English mustard

1 tablespoon *shoyu*

1 tablespoon *sake* **or white wine**

1 tablespoon rice vinegar or white wine vinegar

Cucumber and Persimmon with Sesame-Tofu Dressing

Kyuri to Kaki no Gomadofu-ae

Various types of kaki *(persimmon) grow in Japan. In the fall, when* kaki *is in season, chefs in* ryotei *(formal Japanese restaurants) use it as a decorative garnish appropriate to the time of year. In the West, a smaller variety of persimmon, the Fuyu, is the one to use, as it is still firm when fully ripe. This dish can be served as a non-sweet dessert as well as a salad.*
Serves 4

2–3 Fuyu persimmons

1 English cucumber

For the dressing:

½ x 10-ounce cake firm tofu

5 tablespoons mayonnaise

1½ tablespoons sugar

2 teaspoons white sesame seeds

sea salt

To serve:

salad leaves

1 Peel the persimmons and trim off the stems, then cut each into 8 wedges. Discard any seeds.

2 Cut the cucumber lengthwise in half, then cut each half across, at a slight angle, into ⅓ inch thick half-moons.

3 Arrange the persimmon wedges around the rim of a platter and the cucumber slices decoratively inside, leaving a well in the center for the dressing. Keep the platter in the refrigerator until ready to serve.

4 Press the tofu (see page 29), then put it in a mixing bowl. Mash the tofu, and mix in the mayonnaise, sugar, and sesame seeds. Season with salt to taste. Chill in the refrigerator.

5 Just before serving, pour the dressing into the center of the salad platter and garnish with some salad leaves.

Cucumber and Wakame Vinaigrette
Kyuri to Wakame no Sunomono

Sanbaizu, *a mixture of vinegar,* shoyu, *and sugar, is the most commonly used salad dressing in Japanese cooking. The traditional vinegared salad here, of finely sliced cucumber and* wakame *(young seaweed), can be served as an hors d'oeuvre or as a refreshing accompaniment to a main meal.* **Serves 4–6**

1 large English cucumber

1 teapoon sea salt

⅓ ounce dried *wakame*

For the *sanbaizu* sauce:

3 tablespoons rice vinegar or white wine vinegar

1 tablespoon *shoyu*

½ tablespoon sugar

To serve:

a ½–inch piece of fresh ginger *peeled and finely shredded*

½ **scallion** *finely shredded*

1 Halve the cucumber lengthwise and slice across into very thin half-moons. Spread out on a cutting board and sprinkle with salt. Squash the slices with your hands a few times, then squeeze the excess water out of the cucumber. (Do not rinse.) Put the slices in a mixing bowl.

2 Soak the *wakame* in cold water for 10 minutes or until fully expanded; drain. Lightly blanch in boiling water, then rinse under cold running water. Drain well and squeeze out any excess water with your hands. If the *wakame* is not already chopped, cut away the hard spine-like strip, and chop the soft part into ¾- 1¼-inch lengths. Pat dry with paper towels. Put into the mixing bowl with the cucumber.

3 Mix together the vinegar, *shoyu*, and sugar, stirring well until the sugar dissolves. Pour the sauce onto the cucumber and *wakame*, and toss well. Serve in individual salad bowls, garnished with the ginger and scallion. For a more fancy effect, serve in scallop shells or emptied tangerine cups.

112

Turnip Salad
Kabu Salada

Because of the Buddhist influence, the Japanese traditionally eat far more vegetables than meat. Raw, parboiled, or salted fresh vegetables in a dashi *and* shoyu *sauce are often served as a simple yet very delicious accompaniment to hot boiled rice.* **Serves 4**

1 Cut each turnip into 8 bite-sized half-moons and put in a saucepan with plenty of cold water. Bring to a boil on high heat, then add the snow peas. As soon as the water starts boiling again, drain the vegetables and immediately put under cold running water.

2 Mix the *dashi* granules, *shoyu*, and salt with 1¼ cups of water in a large mixing bowl, stirring well until the *dashi* granules and salt dissolve. Add the parboiled turnips and snow peas to the sauce and leave to marinate for 6–7 minutes. Drain.

3 Heat a small saucepan and toss the sesame seeds over high heat until the first seed pops up. Transfer the seeds to a mortar and roughly pound with a pestle, then mix into the vegetables. Serve in a salad bowl or divide among 4 individual dishes.

8–12 turnips (1½ pounds)
thickly peeled

4 ounces snow peas

1 teaspoon *dashi* granules

2 tablespoons *shoyu*

1 teaspoon sea salt

1 tablespoon white sesame seeds

DESSERTS

AND DRINKS

Rice Cake Wrapped in Adzuki Paste

Ohagi

The Japanese celebrate many ancient festivals, ranging from the arrival of each new season to milestones in children's lives. On such occasions, they often make ohagi, *which are rice cakes wrapped in sweet adzuki bean paste* (an). *You can buy sweet adzuki bean paste, or make your own.* **Makes 10 cakes**

½ **cup (heaped) dried adzuki beans** *soaked for 3–4 hours, then drained*

½ **cup + 1½ tablespoons sugar**

sea salt

¾ **cup glutinous rice**

¼ **cup Japanese rice**

1 Put the beans in a saucepan and just cover with water. Bring to a boil then drain and rinse under cold water. Repeat the process. Finally, put the beans in the saucepan with plenty of water and bring to a boil. Lower the heat and cook for 45 minutes to 1 hour, or until very soft, adding more water when necessary so that the beans are kept just covered.

2 Add the sugar, a third at a time, and a pinch of salt, stirring to mix. Remove from the heat. Mash the beans in the cooking liquid using a potato masher, or purée in a food processor. If the paste is runny, put the pan back on a very low heat and cook, stirring all the time, to evaporate excess liquid. Leave to cool.

3 Wash both kinds of rice together, changing the water 4 or 5 times. Drain and leave to dry for 1 hour before cooking. Put the rice in a cast-iron saucepan and add 7 fluid ounces water. Cover and bring to a boil over high heat. Lower the heat and cook for a further 10–13 minutes, or until all the water is absorbed. Remove from the heat and leave to settle, still covered, for 5 minutes.

4 When the rice is cool enough to handle, use your hands to shape 10 oval balls. Spread about 2 tablespoons of the adzuki paste in the center of a clean damp cloth about 6 inches square. Put a rice ball on the paste, then, using the cloth to help, wrap the paste up around the rice ball. Repeat with the remaining rice balls and paste.

Mochi with Powdered Soybean
Kinako Mochi

Mochi (glutinous rice cakes) make a very good quick snack, particularly for children, as they boost energy and are quite filling. Here they are combined with a mixture of kinako *(powdered soybean) and sugar for a quick sweet.* **Serves 4**

4 tablespoons *kinako*

4 tablespoons sugar

sea salt

8–12 *mochi*

1 Mix together the *kinako*, sugar, and a pinch of salt.

2 Put 4 of the *mochi* in a saucepan and cover with water. Cover and bring to a boil, then remove from the heat. Leave, still covered, for 2 minutes. Alternatively, toast under the broiler, about 5–6 inches from the heat, for 4–5 minutes, or until soft, then dip into hot water.

3 Drain the *mochi* and dredge in the *kinako* mixture to coat all over. Serve immediately (the *mochi* hardens very quickly, so it's advisable to eat it as soon as it's done, without waiting to finish cooking all the cakes). Repeat the process to cook the remaining *mochi*.

Toffee Sweet Potatoes

Daigaku Imo

Although fancy cakes, cookies, candies, and so forth from all around the world are eaten in Japan, the traditional favourites are still very popular. Here's one example. **Serves 4**

1 Cut the sweet potatoes across, slightly on the diagonal, into ½ inch thick oval slices. If the potatoes are large, cut in half lengthwise and then into half-moon slices. (Do not peel.) Put in a deep saucepan with water to cover and cook over medium heat for 10 minutes, or until just soft but still firm. Drain.

2 Heat a large saucepan or wok, and add the sugar and 7 tablespoons water. Heat gently until the sugar dissolves, then bring to a boil and boil over medium heat for 7–8 minutes, or until a light brown caramel syrup is formed. Remove from the heat.

3 Add the cooked sweet potato slices to the caramel syrup and gently toss to coat. Sprinkle with the sesame seeds. Take out the sweet potato slices one by one and lay on a buttered baking sheet or wax paper. Allow the caramel coating to harden.

4 Serve on a platter or individual plates.

2–3 sweet potatoes (1 pound)

1 cup demerara or other raw brown sugar

2 teaspoons black or white sesame seeds

Shochu with Salted Plum

Umeboshi Shochu

Shochu, a distilled wine made from sake *lees,* mirin *lees, grains such as rice, barley, and millet, molasses, or sweet potato, was long regarded as a low-class drink compared to* sake. *However, in recent years it has been re-discovered in Japan, and the fine distillers now all make good* shochu *brands. It is now the most popular drink in Japan, even overtaking Scotch whisky.* **Makes 4 tall drinks**

4 large or 20 tiny *umeboshi*

1 cup *shochu*

hot water

To serve:

lemon slices

1 Put 1 large or several tiny *umeboshi* in each of 4 glasses. Add one-fourth of the *shochu* to each glass and pour in hot water to fill—adjust the strength of the drink by increasing or reducing the amount of hot water.

2 Serve hot, garnished with a lemon slice on the rim of the glass.

Fruit Salad with Kanten and Adzuki Paste
Fruit Anmitsu

Kanten (*also called* agar-agar), *a gelling agent extracted from seaweed, is lighter in texture than gelatin. Fruit juices and purées, sweet adzuki bean paste, and even beaten egg white can be mixed with* kanten *to make molded desserts, or the* kanten *can be made into very simple sweetened cubes.* **Serves 4–6**

½ **stick of dried *kanten*** rinsed, then soaked in cold water for 30 minutes

1½ **tablespoons sugar**

5–7 **ounces canned mandarin orange segments (about ½ can)** drained, syrup reserved

4–5 **tablespoons corn syrup**

1 **small red apple** cored

sea salt

8–12 **green grapes** cut in half and seeds removed

To serve:

strawberries

cream

½ **cup sweet adzuki bean paste (optional)**

1 Drain the *kanten*, squeezing out the water, then tear into pieces. Put the pieces in a saucepan with 7 fluid ounces water and gently simmer until the *kanten* dissolves. (Do not stir at this stage.)

2 Stir in the sugar and continue stirring until it has dissolved, then strain the liquid. Pour the liquid back into the pan and continue to cook for 3 minutes, stirring. Pour into a dampened square mold that measures 3 by 4½ inches and is 1½ inches deep. Leave to cool, then chill until set.

3 Pour 7 tablespoons of the syrup reserved from the mandarin oranges into a bowl. Add the corn syrup, to sweeten to taste. Chill.

4 When the *kanten* has set, cut it into ½-inch cubes. Cut the apple into 6 wedges, then thinly slice each wedge crosswise. Plunge the pieces into salted water to prevent discoloration. Drain and pat dry.

5 Divide all the fruits and the cubes of *kanten* among 4 individual dessert bowls and pour the syrup over. Garnish with a few strawberries and serve with a pitcher of cream and a small bowl of sweet bean paste, to be added individually for extra sweetness and flavor.

Plum Liqueur

Umeshu

The dense-fleshed green plums that appear in produce markets in early summer are used to make umeshu *in many homes in Japan. Essentially a summer drink, it is served chilled over ice cubes or diluted with water. The Japanese also cherish its medicinal qualities in aiding digestion.* Umeshu *will keep indefinitely, but it's so good a drink that it is unlikely to last very long—it never lasted even for a year in my home.* **Makes 2 quarts**

1 Remove the stems from the plums, if using, and wash well. Dry in the sun for about 1 hour, turning occasionally to dry completely. Alternatively, leave to dry out on a windowsill or any airy place.

2 Place one-fourth of the plums, or apricots, in a large glass jar and add one-fourth of the coarse sugar on top. Repeat this three more times until all the fruits and sugar are in the jar. Add the *shochu* and seal tightly. Leave in a dark, cool place, without disturbing, for at least 3 months. The *umeshu* is drinkable after 3 months, but will continue to mature—it's even better if kept for at least a year.

3 To drink, dilute with ice water to your taste, or drink over ice cubes. In winter it can be diluted with hot water. You can eat the fruit as well.

2¼ pounds green plums or apricots

1½ pounds coarse or crystal sugar

2 quarts *shochu* or gin

125

PUBLISHER'S ACKNOWLEDGMENTS

The publisher would like to thank the following photographers for their kind permission to reproduce the photographs in this book.

6 Frank Leather/Eye Ubiquitous; 24–25 Images Colour Library; 64–65 Nigel Blythe/Cephas; 96–97 Paul Chesley/Getty Images; 118–119 C & D Hill/ Andes Press Agency

Also thanks to Hilary Bird, Rachel Hagan, Helen Ridge and Susanna Tee.

AUTHOR'S ACKNOWLEDGMENTS

I am grateful for having the opportunity to compile this collection of popular Japanese recipes, encouraged by Jenni Muir, guided by Kate Bell, and painstakingly edited by Norma MacMillan. I would like to extend my thanks to all my Japanese friends who helped me research recent trends in Japanese street food, in particular Katsuko Hirose, my dear friend of 35 years, who provided moral support as well as a steady stream of cooking information and press cuttings from Japan. Here in the UK, both Lisa Keiko Kirton and Fumiko Nakamura gave me very useful suggestions and actually tested some recipes for me. I also thank many of my English friends and neighbors who acted as guinea-pigs and offered their constructive opinions.